THE TOOLS
they never
GAVE US

Ldwain

Contact Information

/intelligenceoftheheart

www.Ldwain.com

ISBN-10:

0-692-81237-7

ISBN-13:

978-0-692-81237-2

CONTENTS

ACKNOWLEDGEMENTS

There have not been only a few or even several, but unlimited founts of support throughout my life. Everyone that I have ever known, loved, and come into contact with are attributed for my success and continuing legacy. I offer thanks and infinite blessings to all of my family, friends, students, and mentors. May we all continuously grow and achieve the greatest quality of our conscious and sentient evolution.

INTRODUCTION

"It is the supreme art of the teacher to awaken joy
in creative expression and knowledge."

- Albert Einstein

First and foremost, this book is not for *everyone*, but it can be for *anyone* whom chooses it to be so. This is true with all things, but it is not with all things that you will find what you seek. This book cannot be read with merely an intellectual approach. Each word, each line, and each message has been carefully selected.

The primary approach is all about consciously combining what is read with your eyes with what you feel with your entire body. Listening and then understanding in this way is a pure art, and by no means an easy discipline. This book is written in a way that is more raw and succinct then most. Not all of the content is original and some of it may seem original, but truthfully there is really nothing new under the sun. I am just doing my best to convey the same message and legacy of all other masters and authors before me. I humbly ask that you respect the content of this book and enjoy the journey it has to offer. With that being said, let us begin.

All of us have traveled across the hissing and scorching terrains of our psyche. We have faced thunderous and emotional tsunamis upon the sea of our dreams, being blown to-and-fro by the winds of change. We seek and struggle to ground ourselves within precious environments, moving mountains or watching nature laugh at our failed attempts.

Does this mean we give up on these necessary experiences towards self-mastery? The answer should be no, because life is supposed to be filled with adventurous undertakings, arduous endurance, and bold discoveries.

The finest discovery I made was the path of alchemy, the psycho-spiritual journey that lead me out of chaos, into creative expression, and closer to ultimate well-being.

As a sincere individual, do you feel connected to that natural, spiritual, and soulful need of universal understanding? Perhaps you have experienced someone or an event that issued a deep challenge toward you, offering inspiration towards a significant life change. Everything in the universe communicates to those who are sincere and searching for the proper guidance and direction.

The key to universal understanding is through conscious immersion, which is the development of a special kind of awareness. We all have it, but most of us have not activated it. It is the Mind in action, which is made up of the intelligence and the heart or thought and feeling. This is the universal principle that is above and below, within and outside all of existence.

Discovering the natural truth that inspires essential and foundational content of an individual's life is awareness in action. It is the knowing of that Mind that is filled with inspiration, thoughts, and ideas. It is balanced by feelings, emotions, sensations, and intuition. Awareness is the seed of all things and if protected with sincerity it acts as reverence.

This is a necessary respect that allows an individual to see the fundamental pattern of how all outward effects partake of his/her inward nature. This inward nature is the cause to all things. How we perceive and what we do with that perception determines our reality.

Our body is a gift given to us by an invisible force that most know as God, Source, and the Universe itself. However, that gift can also be made into a curse by an individual's own demise. The body and its passages for perception serve as the ultimate tools, demonstrating the proper use of knowing and being. In ancient times the following eloquent words were spoken by a revered, spiritual master who gracefully hinted toward the universal principle mentioned earlier:

"Though seeing, they do not see; though hearing, they do not hear or understand...You will be ever hearing but never understanding; you will be ever seeing but never perceiving."

- Mathew 13:14

Awareness is the aspect of Mind, perceiving is movement of that principle, and faith is the rhythm that continues its universal dance. Most know faith as a divine aspect and it correlates to the inner workings of Earth's soil. Excellent soil yields the necessary nutrients for any seed to grow. Mind is the seed that knows what it is capable of becoming, and we are the instruments that Mind which can sow the seed appropriately. This does not mean that once the seed is placed that all work is complete.

The quality of our consciousness permeates within that seed. As it becomes a seedling, our awareness evolves and transforms with the sprout. This represents the revelation of true focus reaching outward as spirit and manifesting as inspiration. A true attitude of the seedling draws inward as a soulful force and joins in the universal movement of growth.

The spirit and willingness of the seedling yield the grace of life. Remember that faith is the foundation and acts as the fertile soil that is required in the effective use of the Mind. Just as the spirit and soul from the seed manifest in action, those very same forces formed in faith create the harmonic resonance in our body.

There is a significant inward and outward pattern that adheres to the principle of awareness and, if observed gently with great ingenuity, there is no denying the conscious and sentient awareness in all things.

The art of alchemy is the psycho-spiritual process that teaches how to demonstrate and evolve the quality of bodily, soulful and spiritual integrity. It is the art of activating the intimate flow of reality to elevate and evolve the quality of consciousness. Few truly understand alchemy and its relation to all things seen and unseen.

It is a very delicate and sensitive way of transmuting and transforming self-substance, which allows anyone to access gifted awareness and self-mastery. It is a substantial path to unveiling and recognizing the framework of one's own purpose, and the stages of its development.

This book distills and presents practical information, perspectives, and spiritual practices so you can activate your body and awareness, and increase self-mastery. It includes stories about my path to transformation. Here you will find original meditations, introspection, energy work, poetry, fun, activation and so much more!

The purpose of this book is to teach you how to access a healthy and spirited-dynamic way of living through increased spiritual and bodily integrity. It involves the ultimate quest of elevating and evolving the quality of your consciousness!

Allow me to introduce myself. I am the oldest sibling of three, born in Colorado Springs CO, in August of 1988. With my father's career in the U.S. Army, my upbringing was that of a military brat. My family and I lived in Germany as well as other various duty stations throughout the United States. Growing up around different cultures and learning interesting facets of life, I was always questioning the world around me.

At the age of seven I experienced a huge shift in my perspective of the world. My parents decided to split up and not be together anymore. I was raised on Christianity, good values and such, but I did not see how this all tied in to my parents' divorce. This is when I began to question everything that made up my world view at the time.

Nothing was making sense as my emotions were chaotic and impulsive for a while. I slowly began to leave the religious world behind and search where else God could be. Around the ages of ten to twelve I entered into a peculiar fascination of the esoteric arts.

During my junior year of high school in 2006, I received a true form of inspiration while attending theater. This was such a profound experience that I could not ignore it. I was inspired to become a teacher of some kind. Not long after my senior year, I began to be entertained by *angel unawares* at various points. These were all linked to the idea that I was on the right path although my path was not yet clear to me.

I entered into the college scene, trying to find my place in the world, which allowed for me to have a decent grip on reality. I experienced many psycho-spiritual struggles and hardship. It was around this time where I had entered the forest of thorns, trying to discover the Way, the Truth, and the Life that I so strongly had faith in.

With a lot of confusion and still not having a clear direction, I decided to alter the course of my path and joined the United States Coast Guard. Serving only two and a half years, I was honorably discharged for a physiological condition. I even suffered a divorce in between, and was feeling hopeless. Then one fateful sunset I had asked for an absolute renewal of faith. This was my biggest, spiritual shift ever. I am talking about real and sincere, spiritual gut-checks, one right after the other.

Not long after my separation from the military in 2013, and with much deliberation, I transitioned myself into a formal esoteric instruction. With my faith reestablished and my focus and attitude set right, I was back on track.

Within a short period of time, I completed the Alchemy Guild's Certified Instruction Program in Alchemy and Hermetic Philosophy. Having successfully acquired the appropriate credentials, I became an Alchemist & Spiritual Mentor. Through the Alchemy Guild's Certified Instruction Program, I was mentored indirectly under Dennis William Hauk in alchemy and hermetic philosophy.

I completed the rigorous requirements that demonstrated the knowledge and proficiency in both the practical and spiritual aspects of alchemy. From this was formed the qualification to perform psychological and laboratory transformations using the operations from my instruction.

Later, I earned a religious doctorate of philosophy in psycho-spiritual therapy from the Esoteric Interfaith Theological Seminary; along with the ordination of Interfaith Minister from the Esoteric Interfaith Church, Inc. For over fourteen years, my main area of focus has been Christian mysticism, Hermetic principle, and alchemy. The knowledge and instruction contained in this book are from many years of study and practice. These studies have shaped the purpose and mission of my life.

I have always had an ongoing mission to meet a modern vision for inspiring the sincere seekers, teaching them to express a true quality of awareness within a spirited-dynamic manner.

ANSWERING THE CALL

I have always questioned life and the many mysteries it holds since around the age of seven. I was unaware of any spiritual development at the point in time of special occurrence around the age of seventeen. That's the thing though, when such experiences happen they engulf you without choice. This also includes when someone is completely unsuspecting and open to that moment in space and time.

It was the year 2006, I was a junior in high school. I remember being excited about my third period class for theater. I was ready for creative instruction and learning about acting. The side door to the auditorium was opened, and walking through it my stomach filled with butterflies.

Crossing the stage and making my way down into the third row of seats, I was intrigued by the atmosphere and acoustics. The stage appeared intimidating as I imagined performing there one day. Other students began to fill in and soon after that the teacher appeared on stage. His energy felt calm with a strong demeanor, and his voice startled me a bit. I shot down into my seat. With a Bronx, New York accent the first words that exited that man's mouth were, "If you are here and do not want to be, do not waste my time and I will not waste yours."

As he pointed toward the theater exit, a few students were convinced of his sincerity and left. Some seemed unsure and the rest of us looked around to see who else would leave. The room fell silent for a moment. Seconds later the teacher began his introduction on how theater related to life, psychology, and even spirituality. He illustrated his words with seemingly hypnotic gestures, and was convincing the class and myself that life and its entire extraordinary flavor could be integrated into theater.

That's when *it* happened. Boom! In an instant I went beyond captivation and experienced a moment like never before. I felt my entire body and awareness go super nova from within. The atmosphere changed, feeling weightless, and all of the colors of the space appeared more vivid and brilliant than before. *I felt something within me* as my soul was reflecting a specialized focus from the words and gestures of my instructor.

The experience gently forced me to will my presence to be nowhere else but there, simultaneously in an objective and subjective state of being. Filling up with gentle warmth, my body vibrated in its seat. I was in some type of hyper shock, but was extremely serene all at once. Wondering whether anyone was knowledgeable of what was occurring and only able to move my eyes, I looked around and no one seemed to notice. My breath was taken away.

The contours and color of every aspect of my life, every dimension of my being, every thought, every emotion, every moment of happiness, every hour of sadness, every expectation, every hope, and even my doubts were changed in just a few moments. There I was, and when the experience began to dissipate as passing clouds in the sky, the words that whispered passed my lips were, "That's It, I am that!"

After this experience, I struggled for a long time. I did not know what those words meant until I discovered alchemy. It was from this path, whether I chose it or it was chosen for me, that I had learned very valuable lessons. There were times where I had strayed from alchemical instruction, but the universe always reminded me throughout my days to stay true to its purpose. The Way and I had found each other again, but the bridge between the two was master built through recognizing my truths, realization of myself, internalizing and integrating self-knowledge, and understanding and adapting to the new world around me.

All of this may sound great, but as we all know; it all comes with a price. That fee is having gone through, and continuously passing beyond, each threshold where the realm of "shadows" and sleeping "dragons" lurk. They lie awaiting to devour the essence of who we are, unless we come prepared.

THRESHOLD: THE REALM OF SHADOWS AND SLEEPING DRAGONS

The threshold is an invisible realm that has manifested from our denied energies and dreams, and its presence exists to spread out as chaos in our everyday lives. This unconscious realm represents adverse awareness and is ruled by a guardian who controls the entrances and exits. We come across such characters or situations along our journeys toward realization.

The lesser beings of the thresholds are shadows, ghosts, and shape shifters. In alchemy, dragons represent these entities and act as the dark sides of our self. They can be our enemies or allies, and usually these unseen forces try to attract us to the wrong path in life. These guardians represent the force that dwells high and low in all things.

They are the tester of our lives and try to influence our thoughts, words, and actions.

These threshold guardians have even been known to shape shift into the tricksters in religion who dampen our faith, the ignorance of perfect strangers, and the confusing whispers from within. Any and all of its appearances are messy by design and meant to fool and distract us. However, the threshold exists to teach us that it and all that broods there is merely an extension of who we are.

The threshold can be conquered by respect, calmness, and love. Ignorance of this truth is what actually causes the pain and suffering throughout our lives. We put up a resistance for ourselves, being trapped in our own prisons.

Do you remember as a child being a liberated lover and master of imagination? Do you still have the same child-like vigor? Entering the threshold for the first time is when we gave consent to the disparaging poetry in our lives. During the hard times growing up, we directed our energies towards falsehood and depleted our active awareness. We allowed ourselves to become complacent as our connection with all things dwindled.

It seemed as though our *response-abilities*, problems, and difficulties were enforced by the lesser shadows. The sad poetry within us seems irreversible and it overshadows our vigor. We dared not enter the dragon's lair due to chosen fear, because we gave consent for the lack of courage. I have taken notice of these very things about myself and others, perceiving how we deny our lives the right to thrive. Spirit lives within our bodies and is very aware of how we respect what was given to us.

If we continue to stray, that sacred fire within us will sadly leave our bodies hoping to return to its source. Life cannot be lived with our graceful imaginations being shrouded by the threshold. This plane of existence may seem to be linear, matching the course of our lives, but in fact as mentioned before, it resembles the awareness of being. This is multi-dimensional. In our lives we see that the threshold levels may occur as fear, guilt, shame, loss, fatigue, lies, separation, and illusion. The key to subduing the thresholds and the gauntlet of life is developing the ability to perceive with courage and inner strength.

DARE TO PERCEIVE WITH COURAGE AND INNER STRENGTH

Day-to-day life may seem like a giant hodge-podge jigsaw, and being bombarded by all of the trillions of data and information is overwhelming to the real senses. Things may appear to be mundane, boring, routine, repetitive, uninspiring, and tedious.

Does your body feel numb and seemingly placed on autopilot? Looking out at the ordinary world, we think society has tricked us into an ambitious element of conforming. We come back to the idea of existing rather than living. This ongoing stasis keeps us away from fulfilling an innate dormant potential. Walking, stumbling, and hovering in our created, spiritual wasteland provides the comfort to our personas. Wearing such a mask, we cannot accept ourselves and are too afraid of our own truths.

The feeling of an inauthentic life undermines and under powers the authority over our motivations. Being vaguely depressed and unsatisfied, we are left confused and the correct direction to take is another unknown. Some of us might be okay with such sleep, hypnotized away from being. I know I for one out of a multitude do not place faith in such a sorrowful way of life. Doesn't all of this sound absolutely sad? Now trust me, it does not have to be this way.

The need to know who you really are is your right! Be encouraged to ask all the questions regarding your life. Yoda, a fictional character from the *Star Wars* saga once said, "Do or do not. There is no try." Do dare to perceive with courage and inner strength, and do not just be a passer-byer to the chaos found everywhere.

It is very important that you utilize both the objective and subjective realms of reality. Also being equally significant is not clinging to any of the inside and outside effects of those realities. Always seek the cause! For many years we may all stumble upon many confusing subjects, which can send us into a whirlwind of doubt. Only searching outside yourself for too long can lead you into patterns of delusion, nurturing an indulgence of spiritual theory. This sets anyone up for failure, becoming trapped in thoughts of infinite data and information. It is at this juncture that our intelligence can be strung along in a blind fervor.

Remember this, that knowledge is a tool and to be careful of becoming obsessed to the search. Be aware of the lies you tell to yourself and others, of espousing victimization, and entering into a hypnotized, undisciplined quest to *know thyself.*

The key is to restore your faith in the intelligence and heart found within you. Fear will return time and time again to test your courage and strength. Confusion can be occurring themes that will the question the authenticity of your emotional understanding. There was a point in my life where I thought I knew it all and silently this intellectual arrogance crept into all of my affairs, destroying the very things I had promised to uphold. Standing outside one evening during the setting of the sun, I looked out across the pacific sea, and asked for a renewal of faith. I gazed toward the sun, welcoming its warmth and brilliance.

What followed days afterwards was separation and loss, and this confused me further. During such hardship I underwent fatigue and emotional turmoil, and it was affecting a proactive life performance. However, it was these events that were necessary for my self-transformation. I opened my heart to God and received one of the greatest messages ever, and it came from this lesson in scripture:

"...I laid a foundation as a wise builder, and someone else is building on it. But each one should build with care. 11 For no one can lay any foundation other than the one already laid, which is Christ. 12 If anyone builds on this foundation using gold, silver, costly stones, wood, hay or straw, 13 their work will be shown for what it is, because the Day will bring it to light.

It will be revealed with fire, and the fire will

test the quality of each person's work. 14 If what has been built survives, the builder will receive a reward. 15 If it is burned up, the builder will suffer loss but yet will be saved—even though only as one escaping through the flames. 16 Don't you know that you yourselves are God's temple and that God's Spirit dwells in your midst? 17 If anyone destroys God's temple, God will destroy that person; for God's temple is sacred, and you together are that temple."

1 Corinthians 3:10-17

I had been searching for a message like this most of my life, and what I learned was that God manifested its universal spirit and will through the Christ. Why is this important? It is because the incarnation of Christ's purpose was to teach the importance of faith and how it is utilized as a divine instrument. Know this: that faith is the content and foundation of the Alpha and Omega. Without this knowledge nothing can be accomplished. Is it possible to mistreat a foundation such as this? It is certain that the misunderstanding and misuse of worldly knowledge is where the foundation is compromised. The relation of this scripture to alchemy is amazing because the very tool that is used on all levels of transformation is fire, and not only that elemental force. This can be accomplished in the mental, physical, and emotional spheres of existence.

Many times in my life the universe turned up the fire and revealed the truth of my labors by incinerating the lesser existence of habitual nonsense, assumptions, judgments, and relationships. I saw these things and more burn up right before me because of my poor craftsmanship; these creations did not endure the trial by fire. However, it was that very force which inspired the understanding of how to mitigate further falsehoods.

Once I had learned that my body was the temple of a powerful, indwelling presence, I re-answered my calling. Being reminded of the universe's force within my body evolved my sense of respect and awe of all things. Even though the body is crude matter, it still exists as a conduit for the divine. You can access that divinity right now; the opportunity is always there. However, there isn't always the right instruction available to tap into that presence.

In alchemy there is an object known as the retort, which on the mental plane acts as a test tube that is necessary to seal the relevant essences of any experiment at hand. On the physical level the body acts as the same retort, and is the base way of experiencing the chaotic and balanced forces of your life. The objective world of knowledge and your subjective world of knowing go hand in hand, and it is all bitter sweet poetry. Spiritually accepting the quality of faith and quantifying the application of it is the foundation which leads to proper focus and attitude.

The more an individual works with the substance of faith, the deranged *shadows* and terrifying *dragons* will fade away in good timing. The seemingly negative effects of life can be transmuted and transformed into useful resources. Never forget that the threshold cannot be destroyed due to the fact that it is still a dynamic extension of the self. Tend to this aspect of being with calm understanding and respect to its nature, because it too is a part of God.

What is faith, really? Scripture defines is as a substance of things hoped for, and the evidence of things unseen. Courage and inner strength are the things not seen, and are the requirement of entering the *belly of the beast* and *sleighing of the dragon.*

"Now faith is the substance of things hoped for, the evidence of things not seen."

-Hebrews 11:1

The *Now* from the scripture represents the principle of time and part of the unseen which relates to that *now,* the space it occupies. Take notice on the arrangement of words in the scripture. The *now* is perceived as an absolute, and faith follows that constant as a substance. Remember that faith is the content and foundation of life, given to us by a divine zeal. In Romans 12:3 it states:

"For I say, through the grace given to me, to every man that is among you, not to think of him more highly than he ought to think; but to think soberly, accordingly as God has bestowed to every man the measure of faith."

Also, "For it is by grace you have been saved,

through faith—and this is not from yourselves, it is the gift of God."

-Ephesians 2:8-9

It is evident that faith is divinely attributed and is a substance of things hoped for. Hope is our human focus and attitude for things to come; it isn't useless, but not as powerful. Hope is easily turned into self-doubt, self-deceit, and a belief in limitation. It is always in our best interest to direct a certain mindset to obtaining a worthy goal. True faith is unwavering and accomplishes anything. It is backed up by the universal principle of awareness, and having this gives motive to the divine substance.

"...whenever you face trials of any kind, consider it nothing but joy, because you know the testing of your faith produces endurance, and let that have its full effect, so that you may be mature and complete, lacking in nothing."

-James 1:2-4

So, the key to escaping the ordinary is by quantifying your faith. This substance then evolves into courage and strength, which are focus and attitude in action. Knowledge of this substance is great, right? However, just knowing about it and doing nothing with it is almost meaningless. First understand that knowledge is the knowing and wisdom is the doing.

One of my mentors taught me that wisdom is short for having wise dominion over one's self. Putting faith into action effectuates the universal principle, which moves God in us into action. You essentially move from a potential into a vibration, which becomes momentum, and that evolves into a rhythm. Now, courage and inner strength are but a few expressions of spirit. These fiery expressions reveal the true potential from raw vibrations and they animate life, sparking the inner fire within you.

Parts of my childhood are a reminder of the untainted spirit I once had. That very flame inspired amazement and excitement during the times of play and recreation. I have experienced going through life most of the time and giving consent to the sad poetry, causing my directed energies, awareness, and connection with all things to dwindle. Maturity happens, but the allowance of responsibilities, problems, and difficulties overshadowed my vigor. The poetry of our lives reveals so much when we decide to drive backwards to the cause of it all.

Over time, I learned to remove the veil shrouding graceful exploration, and courage and inner strength were necessary to pass through that veil. By the veil I am referring to the threshold. The ability to do so is mastering self-control. The body, when disciplined into an excellent tool, may venture freely without any limitations.

Do you not see how discouraging it is when an unfortunate soul denies their body the right to thrive, ignoring the sacred fire within? Wise meditations bring true stillness to the body and promote the self-control needed for strength. Every moment is poetic and to experience it with true perception invites mastery. Following courage and inner strength is vigilance, which is still held in faith. Bodily truth moves us toward the momentum of creative expression, tapping into the spirit and soul within.

Imagination remains creative, and your worldview will spike due to learning newer things about the people, places, and things everywhere. Keep this encouragement guarded with faith and the threshold will unveil the tools for self-mastery.

"Those who have conquered themselves…live in peace, alike in cold and heat, pleasure and pain, praise and blame…To such people a clump of dirt, a stone, and gold are the same…Because they are impartial, they rise to great heights."

- Krishna Quotes from the Bhagavad Gita

THE RIGHT VIEW VS. THE WRONG VIEW OF MEDITATION

"If you tell me how lofty godliness, prayer, and meditation are to you, I'll tell you how little they are to you."

-Anonymous

Understanding the wrong view of meditation saves us from an overrated and highly misunderstood approach toward wholeness. Having been struck in the gut from what was quoted above; I felt that my view of spiritual discipline, self-security, and comfort as an escape was being attacked. This mentor of mine was not far from the truth, as I was unable to admonish the statement. He helped me to realize the wiser view of the disciplines I had spoken highly of. That was just it. I was only exploiting a topic of delight during the various conversations my mentor and I shared. More time was spent theorizing about my spirituality—exploiting recognition instead of managing my practice.

Realizing that flights of fancy only reveal ignorance, I witnessed that the virtue built up during practice had diminished time and time again. Having analyzed my past habitual meditation discussions and even the speech of others, it seemed that the more meditation was refined in to a mere conversation piece, the less fundamental value it sustained. Although meditation is understood to be a universal practice, it needs to stay true to the art and grace of individual discipline.

From this time in my life, I gathered that meditation should not be placed upon a pedestal, yet the practice needed to be held in respect. Learning this revealed the error of the way I was going about meditation, and this is when my discipline started to evolve. I discovered that meditation is a creative action or inaction and my understanding of it has evolved into disciplined relaxation. The relaxation that set in from my practice helped me to expand awareness, directing attention to the light of consciousness and love of sentience.

I witnessed the share of intelligence and awareness everywhere. A surrendering followed the relaxation, influencing me to let go of the attachments to any residual and unhelpful thoughts. I realized that meditation provided the necessary connection to be aware of the universal involvement. Disciplined relaxation inspired an artful way inside of me. Putting any denied or missing pieces back together, provided me with a more balanced way of living.

The universal principle experienced through meditation even reveals the awareness in the mundane or littlest things we take part in. This principle can be expressed in every step and breath. Being artful with our conscious and sentient awareness helps us to portray our lives as a wonderful mosaic piece of work.

When we go to our place of quietude and meditate, remember to not allow the self to become attached to the fleeting comfort behind closed doors. Disciplined relaxation evolves into a movement beyond the mind, and can represent calmness as power.

CREATING THE SPACE

Every moment is extraordinary. No matter where you are, learning to be calm in realizing the momentum taking place opens the door to more mindful, soulful, and bodily wholeness. Meditation is an ancient activity that is intended to move beyond the facade of falsehood and personality, communicating with the essence of self. It is an art form in focusing consciousness and will. With an alert demeanor, we can direct our attention inward toward cause and then outward for effect. Meditation helps us to evolve and achieve union with our supernal core. The source of this awareness is the same for everyone and closer to us than the breaths we inhale and exhale.

Kabir, a mystic and poet once said, "Student, tell me, what is God? He is the breath within the breath." This saying obviously points to the delightful presence within and all around us. When we breathe, God breathes. When God breathes, the wind blows. When the wind blows the trees dance. When trees dance, the birds sing.

In alchemy, meditation is different from other forms because it is often a *dynamic* process instead of a passive discipline. As an alchemist, I utilize the universal principle and work with the nonphysical energies that exist inwardly. We know these as our thoughts, ideas, imagination, emotions, feelings, and intuition. Do you see how close the *work* is at hand? Directing and manifesting these energies into something truly inspiring is the Magnum Opus (Great Work). The object is not to always still the mind, but to fill it with relevant and chaotic energies, following them back to their source. It is when we misuse the transfer of energies and not labor with them righteously, that the energies unconsciously manifest as adversity in our everyday lives.

In order to work with the levels of reality, we need a space to operate ourselves in. Fortunately for us everywhere we go there we are. Thank you, Confucius! The kind of meditation we will be involved in is active, remember? So everywhere and anywhere you are; this is when the work should be done, and not just behind closed doors. It's best not to go showing off but to keep your meditations guarded with absolute vigilance. This follows the Hermetic axiom,"...To Keep Silent." Trust me, once you go around telling people about your spiritual *design* before it's even completed, the influence of others will add to or take away from what you might have worked so hard for. Remember it also destroys any virtue built up in your process.

What can this process look like? Most meditations incorporate stillness which is only part of the truth. While cultivating stillness, we must also *see* the dark side of deeper essences. We take an introverted journey, penetrating deep into the body and through the soul. Passing beyond the sensory perceptions, we come up against feeling, emotion, will, and intuition. When deeply relaxed, an individual begins to connect with the dormant energies and retrieves them back to their surface. This is where you can begin to explore your sentient awareness.

While exploring the ebb and flow of your sentience, naturally the dormant powers become extroverted within. This means that they start to take on an intangible form, manifesting from the light and consciousness of our thoughts. We can begin to *see* from the inside configuration what is true and what is false. By exposing the latent energies to ourselves, we can use them to purify and increase awareness, vitality, and self-discipline. Merging sentient and conscious awareness together is very powerful in alchemy. We can then take on universal identity, emulating the universal principle. Acquired from this state of being can be freedom from mental, physical, and social restraints.

An individual creates an inner space for meditation that is always active, sealing within it all of the chaotic and calm energies seen and unseen. To the alchemist, this inner platform was the laboratory. More importantly, amongst the alchemist's laboratory test tubes, beakers, and flammable appliances was the retort. This was a glass like flask that you would see used in a science lab, containing all sorts of liquids. The platform was glass to represent the fact that the alchemist could easily see the reactions going on *inside*. I decided to step away from this idea and created a space within that relates to seasons and the elements. I felt that the laboratory and retort idea was too mechanistic for my liking. Having a nature-based space allows me to actually work outside of myself as well in relation to universal principle. Some people choose symbols such as the cross, the yin-yang, sacred geometry etc. Other forms of expression that can be shared with spiritual predecessors of the past are poetry. To keep things simple, the space you can create is a journal.

TO RECOGNIZE

"I love those who can smile in trouble, who can gather strength from distress, and grow brave by reflection. 'Tis the business of little minds to shrink, but they whose heart is firm, and whose conscience approves their conduct, will pursue their principles unto death."

-Leonardo da Vinci

To recognize that the universal principle of awareness is an ever evolving, living thing within and around one's self is essential to living and not just existing. Not to recognize this natural occurrence creates ghosts among humanity. The fork in the road is always present, and you have experienced hesitation in making important decisions of opportunity to *know thyself* as spoken from the

Oracle of Delphi. Some move forward with a decision and others linger in some sort of purgatory for so long, denying their wills and spirits the right to thrive. Purgatory shifts and becomes hell. The notion of just carrying on and unaware of any enthusiasm or inclination is heartbreaking. Just existing is more of a reluctance of recognizing the Way. As we grow up into adulthood, the experience of relationships, emotions, and lessons on living can seem more like a lifelong hardship.

With notions of mere survival and fear, not only do we suffer but the rest of the world around us secretly feels the same. The universe does provide us with signs to not follow deeper into a plight of despair or quiet desperation. The first step to recognizing these signs is listening and opening the eyes to the messages of divine direction. Leveling up your awareness changes the focus and attitude which will lift anyone towards divine inspiration. You will learn to *see* the cause and effect of all things needed to be known, because trusting in the universe reveals the pattern to your life. It is messy by design. Proactive movement in your life will be an example for others to follow. You can show them how choosing to live in truth, not lying to one's self, this is the momentum needed for self-realization.

Poetry is an art form that reveals true feelings from raw vibrations found in words. The quality of consciousness and sentience carried through the words written or spoken is important. The practical use and misuse of these vibrations can animate your life or destroy it. Animating life gives more fuel to the *inner fire*; which is again, spirit. Know that the words in poetry represent the transfer of energy. We can direct the movement of vibration within us and outside of us depending upon the intent of our words.

Journaling is an act of poetry and allows us to work with humility, which reveals the ego. In alchemy this operation is known as Calcination. Starting with the fiery expression in our writings, we can reveal our false personalities by turning the heat up on our personas. This heat is the fire of our consciousness, and in our journals we artfully focus our thoughts, habits, assumptions, judgments and relationships. In your journal, you can even create poetry within poetry from all the things listed above. This is an amazing introspective technique. Reading out loud to your self is another way to transfer energy. Awareness in the words will reveal self-transformation and transmutation in your life. For most people this seems to be a difficult operation to start. Allow me to provide an excerpt from my journal as an example:

"I felt tortured by my dream last night, but then relieved. I was living in my old house up by the light house and it was winter outside. My Wife Marie and I were separated by the connecting house. I knew I was trying to fix us in the dream, because she was so close. Marie and I did interact on some level as neighbors, and it did seem we were getting along well enough to where there was hope in my dream.

"Needless to say, reality is setting in and influencing me to not believe in hope. Marie and I were officially divorced the night before when my roommate handed me the envelope from the court. Reading the letter, I realized it was actually over. The beginning of my dream seemed to taunt me but the universe was showing me a greater way. When death seems to be apparent during winter months, life is revealed during other parts of the year.

"In my dream a sun had risen, brightly. Then it

descended behind distant, rigid, and majestic mountains. The night had come; the air was cold and still. Winter felt present; there was no wind to shutter the dead trees, or to shake the ice sickles that were suspended from the rocky hills. My eyes adjusted to the darkness that surrounded me from a dimly lit moon above. Stars emerged and illuminated their silent melody amongst each other. Ominous clouds formed and roamed into view, claiming the spectacle in the sky. Tears gently fill my eyes as they become more subject to the frigid air. Their liquid began to flow down my face like freezing streams.

"I drop to my knees and begin to whimper into my hands, while trying to clamor for a sense of warmth. I bring my hands down and notice the small splash of tears. The liquid becomes cold and pooled into my palms. Out of nowhere, a snowflake sweeps down into the icy tears, and remains frozen in form. The sky opens up just a little for the moon to shine down upon the tiny object. The snowflake glistens lightly and reminds me to observe the beauty found even in the most cold and sad moments of my life. It is an omen for receiving the new day tomorrow, because I have observed winter diminishing and coming of warmer seasons. I have faith the sun will rise again."

From this dream has also evolved a poem, written as a haiku. This is Japanese poetry and traditionally evokes images of the natural world, and it is one that I meditate on daily. A haiku has seventeen syllables; the first line contains five, next seven, then five again.

With the mind or heart,

Does reality take shape?

In both, truth is lived.

Recognizing Truth

In alchemy, this is where you also begin to work with the *dragon*, but an important thing to note is that as you evolve so does the dragon. There is an alchemical saying, "*Oponere Draconum est prehendre vitam,*" which means, "To face the Dragon is to seize life itself." Once you face this extension of which you are, there is nothing to do but accept it and understand it.

This is without any doubt the most difficult part of

instruction because this is where you will face the lies and falsehoods shared with others and yourself. To recognize your truth and understand the opposing aspects of that truth is the ultimate challenge. In this exercise you will utilize the base level of awareness to isolate and turn up the heat on your persona. This is a very active meditation and requires a great deal of focus and honesty. You will begin to perceive on all levels of truth, including your body, thoughts, habits, assumptions, judgments, and relationships. You are about to reveal a wounded world of known's and unknowns, the denied and self-judged parts of your inferior self. Are you ready to step into the *dragon's lair* to seek and recognize the spiritual fire of transformation?

For this exercise to be effective I am going to repeat that honesty is extremely important, and that at the end of all introspection, define ways to improve your circumstances. In your journal indentify what you like and dislike about your body. What are the strengths and weaknesses of it? Is there pain within certain areas that need healing? What are the lies and truths you tell yourself and others regarding your body? How have you used your body in positive and negative ways? This could mean the use of food, exercise, sexual activity etc.

Now shift your focus to your daily thought patterns. What percentages of them are positive or negative? Identify which thoughts are beneficial or abysmal. Are your thoughts painful or healthy? What are the lies and truths you tell yourself and others regarding your thoughts? Does the use of your thoughts manipulate or offer inspiration?

Next, determine whether you assume or judge against yourself and others. Do you actively gather all of the facts and use them to discern what's false and true? Do you criticize yourself and others? What lies and truths do you share with others regarding the assumptions imposed upon others and yourself? Do you judge or assume out of spite, or are you aware of this disabling ignorance and choose not to do anything to rectify this pattern?

Lastly, place your focus upon all the relationships you have or will be a part of. These include your health, love/social life, wealth, purpose and God/Universe. Do you have a positive or negative relationship to those aspects of your life? How often do you work on strengthening them, or do you passively choose to deny yourself the right to thrive? What are the lies and truths you tell others and yourself in regards to your major relationships? With them do you seek mere recognition or do you strive in the valor of necessary achievement?

This exercise has no time limit because, you need to take your time and give much care over this experiment. If at one point you feel as though you have placed all things upon the mirror of truth, you may go on. It is important that you close the book at this point and work in your journal before moving forward. There is no fast way for true transformation—just the right amount of work and universal timing.

After about a week to two weeks of this experiment you will have recognized a strengthening and special development in self evaluation in your awareness to the people, places, and things around you. You want to always be vigilant for the lies and truths involving your lively hood. Developing this specialized awareness will ultimately help in recognizing your relationship to God/Universe as an advancement in the levels of self-mastery and transformation.

Mirror Mask

This exercise is an advanced method of recognizing your persona and has a creative approach. You will need a few materials to begin this unique meditation:

1) A plain white or black mask from your local craft store or create your own mask using white construction paper, twine, and a hole punch

2) Magazines and scissors for cut outs

3) Markers, paints, colored pencils

4) Other design mediums

Begin designing the mask that represents your shadow persona, the part(s) of your personality which are the lesser substances which seem to control and dictate your life somehow as experienced from the first exercise. Find and cut out from the magazines ideas that may represent the adverse symbolism in your life. Make use of specific symbols, colors, and words that may reflect your challenged state of being upon the mask. Be creative and imaginative as possible in forming this facade tangibly.

After finishing with the design, don the mask in front of a large enough mirror to see most of your body. The upper portion is most important in this case.

You will at least need a solid 10-15 minutes of solitude, without disturbances. Begin to stare gently through the eyes of this design and into the eyes of your reflection. Focus on the eyes and let everything else soften in the reflection. Calmly observe the piece of work you created without judgment or criticism. Begin to accept this vision as an extension of who you have unconsciously chosen.

See the truth of your individuality through the eyes of your hindrance, and immerse yourself into this experience. Be still, because calmness is power. Looking intently into the eyes of your reflection may prove to be difficult or may even seem silly. Such reactions are meant to discourage you. This spawns more fear into your life which weakens your individuality, and this is when your *dragon* may swallow you up. However, once you reach a point of comfort with this exercise, this is movement towards the real you. Integrating this meditation for about a week with the continued bodily awareness is ideal.

This practice needs to be done as many times you feel is necessary. Remember to record whatever it is that you may possibly experience; your goal being to eventually remove the mask for future practices. Do your best not to get lost or give in to any of the effects that may be revealed. Reflect on the cause of this practice only.

From this sort of meditation, you may have experienced very interesting and strange visuals. It's probable to have seen parts of the mask shift and distort in wave like motions, and even seem to dissipate in vision. The gaze of your eyes into the reflection could have revealed a slight discomfort, because this kind of focus is something you are most likely not accustomed to. Other objects around you also seemingly vanished from your view, and the facade could even seem to have animated itself with expression. It was possible to experience subtle dizziness and or vertigo. Evolving your awareness in this way is a key, and it begins to bridge the gap from obscurity to self clarity.

Reflections

Ask yourself this question, have I communicated my

love and appreciation towards a family member or friend today? If you haven't, then ask yourself why not. Family and friends are incredibly wonderful tools. True members of your social circle are the people who accept you exactly as you are. They are meant to be comfortable, accepting, and forgiving. These significant people in your life are the ones who seem to actively care. There exists a specialized bond between you and them, and it is important for you to recognize this. The loyalty and kindness of family and friends are preciously rare.

The world is so busy and densely populated that we often fail to recognize anyone else as a potential friend or acquaintance. Strangers do serve as another important tool, linking us to the world beyond our comfort zones, with mystery and the unknown. They are our unrefined link to God. Another mystery found above us are in the clouds, in ancient times those objects were also indentified with God, and the enigma of its presence.

What moves these graceful objects in the sky is the wind, which is everywhere. Have you ever enjoyed feeling the wind in your face or the sound of the breeze blowing passed your ears? The air moving about is always present, and is likened to the universal principle of awareness.

Signs are abundant throughout your life too. Could you imagine trying to find a restaurant or hotel in a strange location if there were no signs for direction? We are all dependent on them for showing the way. From the ancient days to now signs served a purpose for recognizing the divine and sacred spaces. Sometimes throughout our lives we miss the signs because we were paying attention to what was unnecessary. Do you find yourself so intent on work or useless play that it causes an opportunity for a divine message to not be seen?

Just as there is an abundance of signs, there is also the abundance of water. We know that water surrounds the child within the womb and is the element of cleansing. Our bodies are mostly water and require a constant intake of fresh liquid to continue proper function. We cannot live without this important substance. Water, the most common and essential thing we deal with is a reminder of the daily ritual of cleansing our bodies as a sacral or spiritual use. It is another mystery of life, and science has shown that water, like plants, also responds to specific stimuli too.

Holes, pits, and even graves are identified with emptiness. Have you ever said to yourself or heard others say that "my life is in the pits," which meant life was at rock bottom? Holes can have a positive meaning such as to be filled up with treasures, or seen as a hiding place from danger. Life can be seen as a hole to be filled, and this matches the perspective of seeing the glass half empty, but half filled.

Each day in the earliest part or sometime throughout, make a simple tweak to your schedule and communicate to a friend or family member that you love them and why. When you see a cloud, consider the mystery and awareness of God with humility. Offer a prayer of releasing any limitations you have placed upon yourself or others. The clouds may be distant, but they can act as a reminder of how close God's ways and thoughts are within us. The mystery doesn't have to be obscure. As you go throughout your day, take notice of the wind. Watch, listen, and think of the divine presence within you as the breath of God. As often as you can remember, when you see a sign today, let it be a reminder of the possibility of direction and divine guidance in your life.

Whenever you use water today and for the days that follow, say words of thanks and for blessing the substance into your body. Your life is a potential that can be fulfilled. Try and imagine that you are empty but open to filling your life up with divine presence. If you struggle with emptiness and negativity, invite God and its awareness to transform the despair into something positive and wonderful.

Strangers are a potential for understanding the unknown. Every day, take notice of the people you do not already know. What are they wearing, their speech, and their actions? Imagine what their goals and dreams are, and how they might feel about life. Do not judge or condemn them. Remember that you are as much of a stranger to them as they are to you, and perhaps *their* link to God. The Mind of the universe surrounds us all; ultimately there are no strangers and no division.

Focus on doing these activities for at least week without fail, but you are encouraged to make this a daily habit afterwards. Before you move forward in the book, record the reflections and steps in the journal, and come back after a solid week of reflecting on these things. Record in your journal what you may have experienced in feeling and thought.

After about a week of this experiment you may have recognized a strengthening in your awareness to the people, places, and things around you. Know that there are an infinite number of things to reflect on that can enhance your awareness on a practical level. Do not limit your experiences to the ones listed above, which were taught to me. Personally, I have found that number seven on that list has been the most rewarding of all, and the next chapter will explain why.

PERFECT ENCOUNTERS WITH PERFECT STRANGERS

Who are the perfect strangers to us? Are they the people we ignore when walking on a street side walk, passing them by on our commute somewhere? Maybe we give them a slight glance of acknowledgement; however, the look is seeded with indifference. As passing ghosts, we give little interest and not even a smile most of the time.

Did you know that the disinterest we demonstrate on almost a daily basis manifests as disrespect to the nature within us all? It spreads like a subtle virus and increases the feeling of being unworthy and without consideration. We seem to attempt to give a greeting, such as hello, good morning or how are you. However, these words can exit our lips as clichés. The verbal acknowledgements seem to lack originality and virtue. If your involvement with strangers has been the opposite of the previously explained, well then, on behalf of the universe, thank you.

We seem to live busy lives and often fail to realize opportunities to recognize others as our friends and allies. I have experienced that perfect strangers can serve as an important purpose in our lives of predisposition. The alienated people we come into contact with link us to the mysterious and unknown world beyond our unconscious living.

The world I am speaking of is the one lived with Godly principles. Strangers shall serve as reminders that we are not alone, and they should influence us to be in touch with the universal inside each and every one. There are wonderful examples in my life where unexpected encounters with perfect strangers continue to this day, revealing my link to the universal awareness.

I had been living in San Antonio, Texas at the time of my first contact with a perfect stranger. It was around midnight and the air had cooled down from the humid, hot, and sticky daytime. I was glad that morning was close, because the temperature and weather were perceivably balanced.

Upon exiting a building perched on the top of a hill, I looked up toward the night sky and breathed in the celestial atmosphere. Then looking down, I glanced over the city lights and observed how they mimicked the stars above. I slowly walked from parking lot and on to a nearby sidewalk that was adjacent to the frontage road just a little way from one of the exits. The sounds originating from the city were distant and diffused. Out of all the commotion you could always hear the sirens echoing about, a train whistle bellowing nearby, and the highway murmuring the traffic hum.

I disliked walking on the sidewalk because of being hit by a car there once, so instead I decided to cut through the car lot nearby. The elderly man walking its premises as security took his job very seriously. He would always get after me for taking a short cut instead of walking on the sidewalk. Threatening to call the cops, he would forget my story and every night I would have to explain why strolling through the lot was more preferable. Being a little naive, I could hardly take the man seriously. He seemed over weight and, along with his security button up, he would wear the same brown corduroy pants each time. I do not know, maybe they were really comfortable to patrol in.

Finally making my way through the car lot unscathed, I walked upon the long sidewalk parallel to the apartment complex I was living in. Unfortunately, my building was the one down a steep hill at the very end of the street. You can understand the exercise I put myself through on the muggy days of perspiring torment.

Walking along on the sidewalk; playfully, I hopped up onto a higher curb like we do as kids to test our balance and a man holding what looked like a book appeared to block my path. Stepping down to go around the stranger is when the encounter began.

"Excuse me, but what do you know about God and Christ?" he said. This was not a question I had expected to hear as I made my way in front of this man.

My response was, "Well, I can honestly say that I do not know much about them, besides only having a belief in them." My thoughts were that I was about to be preached at, but I couldn't come up with a reason for escape. I was on my way home but not in a huge rush to arrive there.

"It is a good thing that you believe"—he paused for a breath— "but do you have faith in God and Christ?"

At the time, I did not have a great understanding of what divine faith was and did not know how to respond. My interests fell into things of an esoteric nature, and one of my beliefs was that the Bible was of an exoteric study. I had a general belief that God was the universe and acted in mysterious ways but I lacked the religious view so to speak.

"Well, would you mind learning about God and Christ?"

"Sure," I said, deciding to humor the man.

I found a spot next to him as he opened his book. I knew it was the Bible as soon as I sat down and thought to myself sarcastically, oh boy here we go. Being closer to the man had allowed me to see more of his features. Not much light was present because most of the street lights on that road were out. The man had a stocky stature, dark skin, and a thin mustache with a goatee. He was wearing an interesting jacket with sacred geometry designs, a cross, and an outline of a spiritual light body embedded on it. He did introduce his name, but I am unable to remember. The man opened the Bible up to Colossians chapter 1 and began to read verses 15-17.

"He is the image of the invisible God, the first born of all creation; for in him all things in heaven and on earth were created, things visible and invisible, whether thrones or dominions or rulers or powers —all things have been created through him and for him. He himself is before all things and in him all things hold together."

"Wow, do you see that?" He placed his finger on the page of the scripture.

My thoughts began to move, trying to decipher what had been read to me. I glanced over at the words in the scripture and the man noticed me reading.

"There you go, read the words for yourself. Do you know the *He* that is being referenced here?"

I shook my head.

"The *He* represents Christ..."— a short pause — "Christ is the love of God, but here it also states that out of this love *all* things in heaven and on *earth* were created, things *visible* and *invisible*... Now wait a minute," the man's enthusiasm grew, "Does this mean that out of God's love negative things were made manifest as well? Isn't that something? What do you think?"

I was hesitant to speak, "Uh, well it's kind of a trip. I mean kind of confusing too. But what does it mean by things visible and invisible?"

"Visible are the things we perceive, the things we can experience with our five senses. Things invisible are our consciousness, thoughts, ideas, our emotions, feelings, and sensations. Makes sense, right?"

I nodded my head. "So, when it says He himself is before all things and in Him all things hold together, this scripture is saying that love comes first and holds all things together?"

"You got it."

"Okay, but what about when the scripture says that

God made negative things too?" I paused but then a thought came to me. "I think I get it. Like the yin and yang symbol in Taoism, God also represents universal balance."

"Sounds good to me," the man said.

"Does the Bible always have a deeper meaning to it in all its writing?" I asked this question because of my habit of searching for hidden knowledge in things.

"Perhaps it does." The man smiled.

I was very interested in this encounter. The man and I continued our conversation on God and Christ, relating them to the esoteric knowledge I have come to learn. We bounced ideas off each other for a while, and I started to get tired from being up so late. Our conversation ended and the man had asked if I would pray with him in closing. He said I did not need to be worried about saying anything and that he would lead us in the prayer.

Before now, I had always felt weird about the act of prayer because I did not have much knowledge about it. There had been times I tried praying, always feeling uncertain about it. I do not recall what the man had said during prayer, but I do remember feeling a natural tug inside of me. It was as though something had awakened within, and I felt a vibrating sensation between my heart and solar plexus. After prayer, the man had asked whether I owned a Bible or not and I told him no. He suggested getting one for me but I said it was okay, convincing him not to. The man no longer felt like a stranger and he insisted that if I ever needed a companion in guidance that to visit him in apartment number one.

I understood that he meant the apartment complex I lived in and I was glad to have him as a neighbor. I let him walk away first and I stayed in stillness while sitting. I was doing my best to respect the situation that had just occurred yet not to fall into too much awe. On my way home I decided to call my mom in Oregon. It was about three in the morning her time. I was compelled to share my experience right away and she did not seem to mind. After all she would receive calls from me often during my challenging and exciting situations.

Having described the event I went through, my mother entertained the idea that I was visited by an angel. Listening to this suggestive remark made me wonder if she was right. My mother seemed to share my excitement. I remember walking down steep steps that resembled a terrace when the conversation came to an end. Stopping, I looked up at the starlit sky again and thought, what if?

The next day started off well, and I decided to go pay a visit at the man's apartment to see if what was experienced could be confirmed. It was late morning and the weather was getting warmer. Apartment #1 was another walk all the way up the hill near the main office. I had passed by children kicking a soccer ball around, a little girl chasing a butterfly, and two women on a morning speed run.

Although there were a few clouds scattered throughout the sky, the sun seemed to have missed everyone. As I walked up that hill. I was sweating a little but made my way to shading in front of the man's apartment.

There was a nice welcome mat on the porch and stepping on to it I knocked on the door. There was no answer, so I decided to give a peek in the small side window parallel to the door. Glancing inside, I noticed that nothing appeared to be inside the residence. Standing up straight I scratched my head, thinking huh. I walked away without question and just continued to wonder.

Things were subtly strange for some time and two months after my first encounter another one took place. On my way to take care of the laundry one very early morning, I walked passed an interesting group of individuals. They might have been a little older than me but not by much, and at first glance had an intimidating appearance.

A stereotypical view of these young men would have characterized them as 'thugs'. Being around twenty-one at the time, I walked directly in front of the small group of young men and stopped. Placing the laundry basket on the ground, I introduced myself.

Stepping in closer, I could tell that this group was under the influence of marijuana and alcohol. The young men seemed to be in a calm and relaxed state when they had noticed my presence. One individual was lying on top of a picnic table as three others sat around him. After introducing ourselves, I began a conversation that felt appropriate for their occasion. My intention behind this chance meeting was to bestow an attention to them, which might not have been given to them before. I wanted them to be aware that even a stranger could reach out and communicate some type of universal love. I had meditated on the encounter with the stranger with the bible and on the scripture for a few months, which inspired me to spread this universal message to the group. I could tell that they were all listening very well, and I was glad to become aware of certain synchronicities between them and me.

We all gave each other a turn to communicate what we thought and felt about God, life, the universe, and awareness. I shared my appreciation for these guys having let me introduce myself and speak with them. They felt the same, and at the end of our conversation the group asked for my phone number. These men had convinced me with their sincerity, by stating to contact me just in case one of them needed me to hear them out.

I was glad to give my phone number and then offered them a friendly good-bye. I walked away feeling as though a provision of good service was given. I hoped that this encounter would influence a positive change in my life and at least one individual from the group. Well it did because the following night after getting home from work I received a call.

"Hello," I said answering my cell phone.

The voice on the other side sounded familiar. "Um yea, hey is this C.J.?" C.J. is what my family and close friends called me.

"Yes, what's up?"

"So, do you remember that group you spoke to the other morning, well this is one of the guys that you had given your number to."

"Of course I remember man, what's up?" I was kind of surprised to receive this call.

The young man's voice felt light over the phone. "Well, I just wanted to call and let you know that because of the conversation we had, I wanted to say thank you. Yeah, this is because I was going to do some dangerous things tonight. But when I thought of what was said yesterday, I could not go through with it. So yeah, thanks man."

My eyes began to tear up and my speech was a little wobbly. "Wow man, th-thank you for calling me. I am glad th-that you empowered yourself t-to make the choice you did. Yeah, just re-remember to always give care to yourself and others. Once again, thank you for calling."

In response there was a short pause with a sigh of what sounded like relief. "Yeah man, for real thanks. You take care too, peace out man." The conversation ended.

Removing the cell phone slowly away from my ear and placing it on the nearby table, I began to make my way outside the apartment door. Closing it behind me gently, I looked forward and then up and smiled. I was emotionally moved and felt a deep feeling of warmth with heaviness in my throat. I tried to speak out loud to myself of what I was feeling, but words were unable to express the state I was in.

Tinged with awe, one could only respect what had taken place. Many times over, I have had the opportunity to experience the evolving feelings and sensations of bestowing upon others the universal principal. I have even been open enough to receive the same in return for services rendered. All people in our lives grant us the perfect situations to experience the spark of God and its universal gifts. They can be as subtle as a man standing off to the side of the road holding a card board sign saying, "It could be worse, so why not smile."

There was another time when I was sitting alone in a hotel room, during the depressing time of being separated from my ex-wife. I poured my heart out once again to Christ, God, and the Universe in desperation.

About six months prior to this point, Marie had made the decision to move out of state for the separation, to live with her sister, and to stay there after the divorce. Now I was staying in a hotel near Marie's sister's town, on the verge of signing the divorce papers. I prayed out loud, desperately seeking some sort of sign telling me what to do.

Being so close to Marie after being separated for a long period of time and having limited contact with her made the stay very difficult. I watched a documentary on my computer for the understanding and purpose of life and then I continued to question the meaning behind all that was occurring between Marie and me.

My sleepless night was followed by a day of humility.

I was given the opportunity to prepare a nice steak, pasta, and steamed vegetable dinner for Marie and parts of her family at her sister's house.

I spent about an hour at the grocery store carefully selecting the ingredients for the night's meal. Having completed the task of shopping, I made my way to the rental car to load the food. There was an elderly man walking towards me from just a few car lengths away, balancing himself with a cane in his right hand. As he moved in closer I could tell that the man appeared to be worried about something, and with a low voice he began to speak.

Tears filled his eyes as he held an expression of shame in asking for something. "Excuse me young man, but do you have some food to spare for me to eat?"

I had food but it was reserved for others, and I tried to think of what to say to this stranger. "Look, I do have food but nothing that I can spare because I planned on using it to make a meal for others.

Oh, and besides the food I have is either frozen or completely raw. I also do not have any cash on me to give. I only have my debit card, sorry."

The poor man looked down and began to slowly shuffle away, whispering to himself sadly. I felt remorse and decided to show some compassion. Before the man could turn his back completely the other way, I spoke out.

"Hey, are you really hungry?" I was really curious of his sincerity. The old man nodded and paused in place. The man did appear to be malnourished and in real need of sustenance.

Pointing to the direction behind the man I said, "Here is what I will do. Do you see that fast food restaurant there? Since it is only about a two-minute walk for you, I'll drive over there to meet you for a meal. How does that sound?"

The man showed a little smile as an agreement, but seemed unaware of my sincerity. I told him not to worry and that I would drive right over to the food place. I wanted this man to trust my intent and I did just what I said I would do. Arriving shortly after me, the man seemed a little happy for what was taking place. When we both walked into the restaurant I told him that he could order anything off from the menu. Glancing at the selections briefly he requested a single cheeseburger and drink.

"You only want one cheeseburger? How about you get another one just in case you get hungry again." I spoke to the man hoping he would ask for another burger.

Looking at me he said, "Oh, do you really mean it? Do you mind?"

"Sure that is fine by me." I extended my arm out and patted him on the shoulder.

The man said thank you and placed the order for the extra food item. Moving off to the side while waiting for the order to be filled, the elderly man and I began to connect more. I was surprised to hear what the man had to say. He informed me that he had been homeless for almost six months, and was living under the nearby bridge. I was in the process of losing my wife, and he had lost his wife around the same time Marie separated from me. I was able to empathize with the man because even though I had a place to stay, without my wife I felt homeless as well.

"Yeah, I am going through a divorce soon. I visited Texas in order to have the papers signed and to give a last good-bye to my wife." I was struck again with sadness.

The old man said to me softly, "Oh, do not worry. You are a good man, I can see that. I just want to thank you for your kindness, young man. God bless your soul, Jesus would have appreciated what you have done today. What is your name so that I may pray for you, if you do not mind me asking?"

I felt that the moment he and I were sharing was precious and almost indescribable. The gratitude emanating from this man was of an immense measure. My eyes began to water due to the compassion the old man and I were sharing.

"You and I know that things change for what's best for us," the man said.

I nodded in response and then the food was up. Ushering the man out the door was humbling. He thanked me again, smiled, and began to walk away from the building. Looking down at the ground, I thought wow. I remembered about last night when I had prayed for the sign, yet it was still hard to believe what had just occurred. So standing there in awe, I threw my head back in laughter. With my eyes still a little watery, I wiped away their extra moisture and made my way to the house of Marie's sister. Just so you know, the meal did go well and the night ended calmly.

SENSITIZING, SOFT GAZING AND QUIET NURTURING

Self-control is strength, and it takes courage to develop. This chapter describes exercises that will enhance awareness of your body, the material world, extend your awareness of the unseen, improve your physicality, and finally your ability to relax.

The Five Senses

The first tools you are to work with are the senses

because they are the filters that take in all of the data and information. It makes sense to activate the physical body and its passages of perception in order to develop the ability to make instinctual a connection to the unseen. All that is essential is invisible to the physical senses because most individuals are used by the physical senses instead of mastering the use of these tools.

Sight

I would like for you to begin working with the sense of sight by looking all around you and identifying what you see. I recommend going outside in nature or a busy location and immerse yourself in what you are seeing in the environment. Describe quietly to yourself or in thought all of the colors, shapes, sizes, and movements you are experiencing.

For example, go to an active park with lots of people doing various activities such as walking their dog, playing some sort of sport, laughing, changing their facial expressions etc. Look at all the detail in that location. Watch to see the wind gently breeze through the trees, birds flying from branches, clouds roaming calmly above or notice brilliant sun patches throughout the area. Not attaching yourself to what is being observed, make this silent statement, "I am what I see, and I am sensitizing my sense of sight to enhance my awareness and perception of seeing."

Also during the night times when it is dark, notice the difference in appearances while lying in bed. See how the environment contrasts the lightness and darkness of the visuals, and repeat the same statement from above.

Here are some other important examples to follow:

Wake up early enough to observe the sun rise and see how the sky is slowly painted with various textures and colors. Become fascinated with the morning dew which glisten rainbow shimmers throughout the grass, as the sun provides amazing visuals shining through trees, revealing seasonal, aura patterns. Watching the effects of water and rainfall is special too because it causes various surfaces to ripple, creating concentric designs. Sit and watch a flame dance gently from a candle wick or actively wave in a bon fire.

Touch

Next is your sense of touch. I recommend you experiment with this practice in a nature setting. The reason for this is because the energy of others, whether negative or positive, is transferred to a tree upon touching it. The tree knows how to recycle, displace, or use that level of transfer accordingly. Touching objects such as door knobs, tools, or other things used by people can have a displeasing effect while consciously doing this sort of exercise. When different levels of energy are transferred into those kinds of objects, they do not have the same ability to do as nature does.

Let's say you are at the park again, and as you walk through it, touch the trees to experience the textures. Reach out to a leaf and feel its softness or roughness. If the wind is blowing, experience whether it varies in warmth or coldness. As others walk by you are the vibrations of their steps being felt underneath your feet?

Or perhaps you go to the beach and run your hands through the graininess of the sand. As you are doing any of this, say quietly to yourself or in thought, "I am what I feel, and I am sensitizing my sense of touch to enhance my awareness and perception of feeling."

Taste

Every time that you eat, take an extended amount of time to immerse into the flavorful experience. Are the foods being consumed salty, sour, bitter, sweet, hard, crunchy, soft, gooey, or in liquid form?

Practicing your sense of touch with the sense of taste is helpful too. As you take in each substance say to yourself in thought, "I am what I eat, and I am sensitizing my sense of taste to enhance my awareness and perception of flavor and texture."

Hearing

As you are in your chosen environment also identify all the types of sounds you hear. Birds may be chirping, wind breezing through the trees, children laughing, people walking, cars driving, horns honking, rain falling, thunder roaring, late night calm, or a quiet snow fall.

Whatever the sounds may be, take notice of the distinct variations. Say to yourself quietly or in thought," I am what I hear, and I am sensitizing my sense of sound to enhance my awareness and perception of hearing."

Smell

For your sense of smell pick up on the various aromas in the environment. Perhaps you are at a movie theater and smell of popcorn fills the air. Maybe you are at the beach and can smell the stale or salty ocean breeze. When cooking, take notice of the colorful scents lingering from the delicious foods.

I recommend doing this practice for delightful or welcoming smells, and I don't think I need to go into detail why. As you pick up on the abundance of aromas say to yourself quietly or in thought," I am what I smell, and I am sensitizing my sense of smell to enhance my awareness and perception of smelling."

Deepening Your Connection to All Your Senses

Remember to connect sincerity into what you are declaring; it makes a huge difference in developing awareness beyond the physical senses. Practice this intently for at least an entire week for each sense. Record any and all of the experiences in your journal. This will get you started. But remember that this is a life discipline. I recommended you practice enhancing your senses continuously throughout your life.

Enhancing your senses at this level opens the door to many advanced functions of your spiritual perception. After having gone through an entire week or so of this practice and staying true to its applications, you may have experienced very interesting shifts with your five basic senses.

The goal here is establishing a foundational level of clarity with your base understanding of how to put in to use the passages of perception. If you really want to have a deeper connection to your senses, try over lapping them with feeling. This is more like feeling within the feeling and knowing that you know how to sense what is seen.

For an example, feel with your eyes as you view the various colors, shapes, sizes, and textures of your environments.

The more aware you become of the limitless amounts of data taken in by the senses, the more things you may begin to see that may not have been present before.

Disciplined Relaxation

First find a quiet place for some solitude that has a sturdy chair with no arm rests. Sit up right in the chair, but position your body almost close to the edge. Rest your hands face down on your thighs, with your shoulders relaxed. Allow your breathing to rise and fall in a gentle rhythm. Inhale through your nose, and let your breath slowly fill your belly. Then exhale through your nose, pushing the air completely out from your belly. Repeat several times until you feel relaxed.

You can think about anything but do not let your eyes roam around the setting. Keep your eyes open and relaxed at first then later try to sit with your eyes closed but still relaxed. Try not to move at all for about fifteen minutes and within this time, you may notice that your breathing starts to dissipate. Naturally, your breath will take care of itself for you to enter into a true, calm state of being.

Now shift to a soft focus. Have you ever heard of *the thousand-yard stare?* This is something in the military you learn to do in order not to break bearing during a uniform inspection. It helps to stay away from an acute focus and instead shift to a soft and distant focus. In art there is a technique called "cloud technique" which is used to soften up any hard edges of a still life the artist is observing. This makes it easier to see shapes only.

Naturally our eyes stay in a single point focus and we tend to zoom in on certain focal points of objects that are seen within the environment. Soft focus widens the view and allows us to see into the peripherals better. If done correctly, you will notice that the soft focus seemingly brings your environment to you instead of sending a sharp focus outward.

In the figure to follow, there is another way to tell whether you are focusing your eyes softly enough for future meditations. Looking at the shape on the next page, study the outline for a bit.

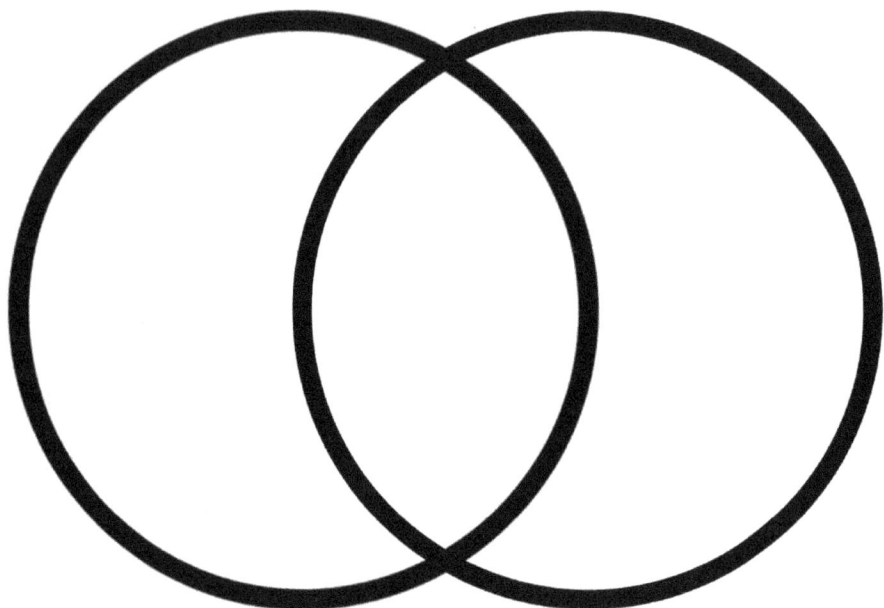

Are you able to only see the two crescent moons touching? If not, relax your eyes to where you are just focusing on the outline of the shape above, forming only the image of the two crescent moons. Now, switch back and forth between the whole shape (the two circles) and the moons. Try to really feel the difference between your acute focus and soft focus and train your eyes to receive the sensations between each visual switch. Seeing should be a felt practice not just a passive reception.

Within the fifteen minutes you may experience certain parts of the body twitch or even jerk. This is normal, and represents residual restless energy trying to move about. Some have said that this may also represent the *kundalini* energy awakening up the spine.

Apply these disciplines for at least a week, and day after day try to inhibit thoughts. You will begin to experience a different kind of relaxation. While inhibiting thoughts, start to feel your body and any sensations occurring. At this point you can practice this sitting with eyes closed. Record the experience in your journal.

Having done the first week of this practice furthers the discipline of bodily awareness and will allow you *see* what *stillness* is all about.

Giving Awareness to the Body

The following practice advances your bodily awareness and the beginning of self-healing. Each day as soon as you wake up in the morning (or whenever your schedule permits) work on stretching the body in various but safe ways. Try not to strain, but instead *push* your body gently. Another must, is to train your hands to massage your body where ever reachable. As you do this, focus on the awareness of what your hands are feeling.

Make sure to thoroughly massage the center area of your palms, and rub them together in a prayer like gesture to generate heat and warmth. This is important because it enables the sensitivity of future energetic experiences. Sense the cold on your body all over before the touch and then sense the warmth afterwards.

A tingling sensation will most likely occur if you are really working the massage. This helps with blood, water, and energy circulation, and even strengthens the muscles in your hands. Doing this is an easy way to move the spirit within you, increasing vitality.

After about a week of continual relaxing of the body, you need to be very familiar with how your body feels all over: where it is cold, warm, tingly, rough, smooth etc. Record the experience in your journal.

You will come to see how you are advancing along in your practice of giving more awareness to the body. Stay on track and allow yourself to enter an advanced stage of sensing or body scanning.

Stopping and Seeing

This is another type of exercise that is simple and very direct and should be incorporated with all of your movements throughout the day.

Let's begin with the morning. With this exercise, try to wake up early enough to give yourself the opportunity to experience your morning consciously. Before you open your eyes, greeting the day with your vision, stop. Open your eyes with the awareness that you are doing so. Almost dramatically, slowly allow the daylight to pierce you awake. Take a good look around, and feel your environment. Overlap all of your senses with feeling. Before you move, become aware of the choice to do so. Slowly follow through with your movement, gently hanging on every adjustment.

Observe the choice to plant your feet down and then do so. As your feet touch the floor, stop. Is the floor cold or is it warm? Sense the textures on the bottom of your feet and curl your toes into the surface.

Be vigilant of your next decision and stand up with

the awareness to execute movement. This next part will be very interesting, because it's probably something you have never done. Make your next movements in slow motion, being almost dramatic, and staying aware of each step as it happens.

Every time you enter a new environment of your house or place of stay, stop and *see* your movements and relationship to the environment. When you reach for objects, watch your hands motion toward them. You are feeling the presence of movement. It may seem silly, but this disciplines and evolves your awareness even further. Try practicing different speeds of movement, but safely.

Not only be acutely aware of the movements of your body, but also of your thoughts and words. Speak slowly and gently with your disciplined awareness. See how the quality of any moment reflects the quality of this principle.

Stopping and seeing pulls you skillfully out of the hustle and bustle of daily activity. You will feel more in control, but understand this is not absolute. It is only directional control, so do not obsess or over analyze each movement. This is a practice in being graceful, enjoy it.

Record all experiences in your journal.

After having practiced the previous meditations myself, I subtly entered into the theme of advanced awareness. While being prompted a long while back to sensitize my senses and visualization skills, I was always on the edge of something new. Off and on I worked with my senses and each time I allowed full awareness, I saw, felt, and heard very strange and peculiar things. Without a doubt, there is a force that exists on both tangible and intangible fields of existence. With everything that you think, say, or do, this principle can be felt.

Beginning of Energetic Body Scanning

After having felt the cold, warmth, and tingling of your body, you will now advance towards energetic body scanning. Continue the session with raised hands slightly above the skin. Do this for about fifteen minutes or so, sitting at first and then standing. Begin to move your hands over the body in slow Tai Chi like movements. With your hands strengthened more circulation flows through them, which means more energy flows through them. Match your breathing to the gentle movements, but play with it as well.

When standing, remember to breathe from your heels up as slowly and gently as possible. Remember not to force the movements or breathing, but just settle into each with continued awareness. Keeping your awareness in your hands, try to sense the temperature variations at this distance.

You will notice that you are beginning to move energy all over your body. Inhaling up from your heels to the top of your head and exhaling down the spine with the breath, you will notice warmth filling up the front of your body then back through your spine and down to your heels again.

Also, try moving the breath up the spine and down the front and experiment with those movements. With this kind of movement, you are creating a water wheel effect of energy throughout your body. In between each movement, do yourself a favor and come to a point of rest, placing your palms together in a prayer position close to the body. Later on you will learn why this is such an important gesture, beyond what you may already know from prayer.

Continue disciplining the body this way for another week or so, and you should experience more than just temperature variations. Static electricity and even a magnetic flux feeling can be subtly felt. Sensing these subtle variations will come in *handy* with more advanced energy work later on. Record your experiences in writing. Extending this practice daily will help you gradually cultivate vitality and energy which is life. Bodily awareness is the path to your well-being.

Activating Your Biological Systems

Continuing with bodily awareness techniques, it is equally important to discipline your focus on the four major biological systems: reproductive, circulatory, respiratory, and digestive.

Reproductive System

Find yourself in a comfortable, quiet environment if possible. If you are unable to be alone, then this advanced focus technique is suitable when others are around, such as when you are commuting on the bus, sitting at work on break or in this midst of a loud event. As appropriate, you may lie down, stand or sit up, but keep an erect, relaxed posture. Close your eyes and put all of your awareness down into your reproductive region. Circulate your attention between the different areas of your lower pelvic area.

When you inhale, bring a deep breath into your belly and hold for 4-6 seconds. Now, exhale your breath, placing the awareness of dropping your air into your reproductive system, feeling the warmth and other sensations that might occur. After the exhale, inhale deeply once again while tightening the muscles that make up your pelvic floor and hold. This action is the equivalent sensation of stopping and releasing your urine.

Keep your awareness in your reproductive system as you feel your belly fill up with air once again. On the exhale, relax the pelvic floor muscles. Repeat this exercise 4-6 times in one sitting, but as often as you can.

Circulatory System

For the circulatory system, repeat the beginning steps from the previous exercise, but instead place your focus on your heart. While breathing, see if you can feel your heart beat and the inside warmth. Stay with that sensation for a few minutes or so. See if you can trace the warmth of your heart throughout the various parts of your body. You might feel your skin tingling from the awareness being placed throughout your venial network.

Consciously sense the very subtle flow of your blood within. After tracing the warmth all over for about 5-10 minutes, return your soft focus to your heart and just be present with it for another 5 minutes. This exercise should last for 10-15 minutes or so, and can be repeated anytime.

Respiratory system

For your respiratory system, keep practicing the rhythmic breathing suggested from the earlier practices. This is when all you need to do is relax and feel into the breath with your enhanced awareness.

Digestive System

For the digestive system, my suggestion is that your eating habits should consist of taking in simple foods and drinking as much as possible. This definitely means fruits, vegetables, yogurt (Greek), water, juice, and healthy proteins. The simpler the food, the easier the digestive breakdown and absorption of the proper nutrients will be. Here is another important note: consuming food or drink colder than room temperature makes it harder for the stomach to produce the necessary amount of acid for proper digestion. Always maintain a gentle focus whenever you are hungry.

When eating, keep a soft awareness on the foods that go into your mouth. As you chew your sustenance, do so gracefully. Pay attention to the varying nuances from the food. Also if you can, allow your food to be broken down so it is very easy to swallow.

When swallowing, feel the sensation of the food descending down the throat and into the belly. Next, take a deep breath through your nose, filling the stomach up with air, and then exhale slowly. Food is a gift, and such practices influence gratitude.

Final Recommendations

It should be obvious why you want to make all of the aforementioned disciplines part of your daily life. However, a solid week needs to go by for each exercise before continuing further. Do not let these practices only be part of your morning and nightly routines, but integrate them throughout all parts of your day. Take the time to record the experience in your journal.

Be skillful and creative in the use of activating your physical body, because these exercises are effective tools toward self-healing. Respect and give care to your body always, which is part of sustaining the universal principle. Know that power is *felt* in calmness, and especially the calmness of breath and movement. Being able to transfer that power into your daily activities and relationships is very important.

If you have been successfully recording in your journal all of what you are experiencing, expressing yourself in such a way begins to allow you to determine reality differently than before. It is true that change in your life is obvious, but being aware of that change unfolds the miraculous.

TO REALIZE

Diving deeper into awareness accesses inner knowing and begins to form that knowledge into wisdom. An incorrect pursuit of knowledge leads into many patterns of delusional circles. As that happens, an individual is snared by an over indulgence of information and not enough practice. Instead, a drone is born, adapting victimization and a hypnotized search.

The watery world of emotions is the key to a deeper, dimensional authenticity. Emotional discipline flows with vast alertness. Water's calm expression aides a center of balance between expressive attributes, influencing peace, and ushering a sincere transformation of the self. In alchemy, this operation is known as dissolution. You can gain control of the *Dragon* by the further breakdown of your personality and immersion into your primal level, your soul.

This is when you surrender yourself to your inner presence and this is hinted at in scripture:

"Be still and know that I am God."

-Psalm 46:10

In alchemy surrender is known as this: "There is only one way to survive the Dragon. Be still. Rest in the arms of the Dragon."

Diving into the dark waters of our unconscious Mind is the stage of purification. The idea also relates to being baptized in Christianity:

"When He had been baptized, Christ came up immediately from the water; and behold, the heavens were opened to him, and He saw the Spirit of God descending like a dove and lighting upon Him..."   -Matthew 3:16

Just as Christ was baptized from the water; we dive

into our awareness to purify the personality. At this point we have to acknowledge the chaos in the world and within ourselves. We must suffer through the acceptance of our good and bad, positive and negative, life and death, and many other poles of existence.

We exercise this by directing our adverse emotions in to the light and not allowing an unconscious bearing. In alchemy, we know this as rising above the "poisonous vapors" of the subconscious and learn to merge the dark side into a spiritual self. This is where you will see the messy by design pattern.

As you are internally experiencing this transformation, record and relate to the fact of *slowing down* and paying attention to feelings. Really feel the emotions you experience, but do not become them.

Dissolve

At this stage, you also need to work with denied or suppressed energies of emotions you may have pent up. Here are some of the emotions to become aware of:

· Guilt

· Shame

· Sorrow

· Doubt

Having already taken the leap of faith by inviting strength and courage into your life, using awareness we can now concentrate and dissolve these emotions. Adverse emotions are the way we judge or have judged ourselves and others. Releasing and *letting go* frees those trapped energies of mental/emotional habits, stiff beliefs, and projections.

With each adverse emotion, write and speak out loud an affirmation that is unique to you that will release that emotion. Also, match each emotion with a positive message, but remember to put gentleness in their release toward serenity.

I recommend that you do the breath work described below with each affirmation you choose to work with.

Inhale deeply and slowly into your belly, gently hold for 4 seconds, and exhale deeply from the belly for a count of 4 seconds. Then say one of your affirmations. Then inhale deeply and slowly into your belly, gently hold for 4 seconds, and exhale deeply from the belly for a count of 4 seconds.

Example Affirmations

"I am the loving release of the guilt that I have judged against myself and others."

"I no longer choose to deny my guilt but instead to dissolve it within serenity."

"I am the forgiving force, releasing the shame of foolish tendencies."

"I no longer choose to deny my shame but instead dissolve it within serenity."

"I gently accept and release the sorrow and suffering I have put myself through."

"I no longer choose to blame myself for any loss I have encountered."

"I kindly dissolve my distress within serenity."

"The truth within me releases any doubt caused by

patterns of self-deception and the practice of deceit."

"I choose to express myself honestly and give no more lies to myself or others."

"That truth within me dissolves doubt within serenity."

Do this practice each day for about a week. Try finding other emotions that need dissolving. Glide gently over each word and feel the significance of their presence and placement. What are the feelings and sensations that you experience doing the breath work for your statements? Did you really connect with the process of breathing and releasing the emotions? Record in your journal what you experience. Keep in mind that this way of practicing the breath consciously allows the body to oxygenate itself more effectively over time.

After a week of this practice you will start to realize a deeper awareness and connection to your soul at a base level through your breath and emotions. Going further requires more effort and advanced exposure.

Dark Waters

Here is an advanced practice to dissolve your feelings of discomfort in a way you have probably never consciously experienced. This practice suggests the further breaking down of your persona, and consciously enters you into the watery world of emotions. I will point out once again that this kind of meditation can reveal deep-seeded discomforting imagery and feelings. However, I will provide an idea that will be a stimulus of possible comfort and balance.

By now, you have faithfully reached a certain level of comfort and confidence with your body and are ready to venture further within. This exercise should be performed in a completely dark space, preferably at night, and without disruption. If completely alone, perform this meditation with as little clothing as possible; the more exposure the better. Plan for about fifteen minutes at first. This will be sufficient for a while. Then increase the time gradually, eventually having the number of minutes you meditate equal your age.

For the positive stimulus, have some gentle, quiet

music playing in the background. The music is there to keep you anchored to the cause of the experience because you will be participating in absolute darkness. Your eyes should remain open the entire time. If you fear the dark, this meditation will expose you and eventually move you beyond that fear.

Sit in a comfortable position on the floor or in a chair, placing your body in the center of the environment. Your back should remain upright and comfortably erect. Make sure you can safely move around and about for preparation and ending. Do your best to stay focused and not to lose heart. This is your conscious experience of immersion into the darkness of your unconscious.

Remember when I had mentioned the importance of the prayer gesture? This is significant because it not only creates a closed circuit of energy and balance, but it also protects you from outside influences. I am referring to the scary and discomforting energies that may be experienced with this meditation.

Also, remember that all you will see and feel outside of you is indeed an extension of who you are. As you rest in the darkness with eyes open, you are working through sensations and feelings. Your breathing should carry the discipline you have developed during earlier practices.

You are working to bring darkness to the light of your being by accessing your soul. This is skillful polarization. Observe, listen, and be aware. The *dragon* is watching you. Be still; the gentle music along with the prayer gesture are your protection. Once you have surpassed the fear and other lesser feelings, you have risen above the *poisonous vapors.*

This represents rising to emotional control consciously entering into your sentient awareness. From this point, you are learning to integrate your shadow victim into authenticity. With eyes open shift into your soft focus. This will calm your environment and open your vision to the subtle energies all around you.

Moving passed the surface shadows; you can now begin to *see* in the dark. You may perceive dancing colors in the form of dots/orbs moving like a flock of birds, kaleidoscopic imagery, electrostatic energy, and luminescence. These are all the appealing side effects for tapping within your environment skillfully and calmly. Try not to get lost in them and stay true to the cause of your experimentation.

Conclude your session by closing your eyes for a few moments and bringing awareness back to just your body. Soon after, open your eyes, get up safely and find your way to the lights. It would be better to have a candle and match nearby for a softer adjustment to the lighting.

Do this exercise at least three times each week and record the experience in your journal. Perform this meditation until a complete level of calming discipline is achieved and your fear of the dark is lessened.

The *Dark Waters* meditation is a challenging practice. The point behind it is the feeling of exposing yourself to the dark side of your soul through the feelings you may have experienced during the exercise. Darkness is just as much of a tool as light is, and building a relationship to both will increase your awareness greatly.

In your experimentation through specific meditations, you may see and feel sort of a blanket of thickness, soft and flexible, invisible to normal vision.

While utilizing a soft-focus technique and observing your surroundings, vision can reveal things as moving static.

The reality around you can move around in wave-like movements. From the *Dark Waters* meditation, you may have a continued experience, seeing ghostly circles, triangles, and squares. Sometimes colorful orbs float around, as you may have experienced from the dark water meditation. As your soft focus becomes increasingly relaxed the shapes disappear, forming into straight and squiggly small lines of light. These will appear to move about in a thin, dark purple fuzziness.

The deeper you enter the realm of meditation with eyes open, sparks and pops of colorful lighting may be perceived. Your vision can fade out, and you can feel as though you have entered into a very conscious dream state. What you see all around you may dissipate and vanish; all that remains is just a feeling. It is a sensation of absolute being; you become an observer of no-thing, returning to a void. It is quite an interesting experience and worth experimenting with often.

Heart Pulse Transfer Meditation

With this meditation let's start to bring our enhanced awareness into our bodies and work with the heart.

As always, find a quiet, comfortable place to begin this practice. Do your best to avoid distractions. You will need ear plugs or use your palms to cover your ears for the first part of this practice. The ear plugs (or palms) are for familiarizing yourself with the unique sound of your heart beat.

This time you will stand in the center of your space, if possible. With ear plugs in (or palms covering your ears), place yourself into a relaxed breathing state, keeping your chest up, your butt slightly and comfortably tucked under the spine, and your feet shoulder width apart.

Again, keep your eyes open and get into that soft-focus gaze. While breathing gently, listen to the sound of your beating heart by focusing on its native area. Take notice of its rhythm and specific pound. Sense the stillness between each palpitation. Immerse your awareness into this experience for about five minutes or so.

If you have not yet acquired ear plugs, this next part will be difficult to do. With ear plugs still in, place your dominant palm over the area of your heart, overlapping with your other palm. Now, listen and feel the beat of your heart. Familiarize yourself with the sensations even further for another five minutes.

Next, remove your hands but stay aware of the sensations, feeling your heart without your hands. It may be subtle but it's there, just feel it. Keep this presence for another five minutes or so. Your heart beat does not just exist in its physical location. It can be felt all over your body as I have stated before. Try moving your heart beat awareness to various parts of your body and sense it. Eventually, you will be able to feel your entire body pulse altogether.

Try to do this meditation daily or at least three times a week. Record what you feel and see in your journal. Once you have achieved the level of sensing your heart beat pulse all over, try to extend this feeling into the space around you.

It will be very possible to sense your entire space pulsating with practice. If this is something you can accomplish, advanced methods of this practice will be less challenging.

After practicing with the transfer of your heart energy you may experience the data of your pulse being sent out in colors. There are various times when practicing the above with my eyes open that I saw purples and greens pulsating outward from my beginning field of vision. Sending my awareness out with and into the colors, I received the sensation of tugging and pulling.

The larger my environment, the greater the effect was. If you ever can or deem it appropriate, do not limit yourself in any of these practices. Being out in nature, whenever possible, has yielded more interesting outcomes than keeping yourself in a box of some type. It's important to know that cubes actually keep and trap our energy in a way that solidifies the movement and flow. It's only when we make the conscious effort to penetrate beyond the box, *thinking outside the box*, life becomes increasingly profound.

Sound of Silence Meditation

You can perform this practice right before you lie down for the night or very early in the morning before anyone else wakes up. Anyone else could also mean the majority of your neighborhood. This is so that there will be a lesser amount of anyone else's surrounding energies influencing this experience because they are still sleeping. Sitting or lying down comfortably is ideal.

Repeat the previous heart transfer meditation up until you place your hands on your chest. Or place your hands in the prayer gesture, resting upon that area. You will notice your breathing slowing down significantly as well as your heart beat. Try not to be alarmed of this. However, if you feel uncomfortable continuing then stop. Your awareness of the sounds of the environment will increase, some louder than others. You are to filter passed those sounds. It is best to identify them consciously, for this will eliminate the need to figure out what you are hearing.

After a certain point, you will begin to hear all sounds fade away into a hum. The hum will lessen and then what follows next is a hissing or piping noise that covers up all the sounds heard throughout the house, including your heart. The hush can fluctuate between the hissing and hum.

Wherever you are, you will feel your body drop slowly into a silent descent sensation. It may seem like heaviness, dropping you into and through the bed, chair or even the floor. You will pass through that thick blanket I mentioned earlier and the sensation may eventually vanish. However, if you stay with the experience down the *rabbit hole* you may go.

You will have a tunneling sensation in vision and feeling altogether. It's very possible for you to just fall asleep, but as you stick with the experience more can occur. You can end the session by purposefully falling asleep or by humming your body awake. I found that by buzzing like a bee helps. In fact, this was taught to me in a dream.

Have fun with this exercise and practice it nightly or early in the mornings. Eventually try to sense that silence in any situation and environment. Record what you find in your journals; make sure you are consistent with its entries.

If you choose to continue, you may remain awake but feel asleep. Your body may feel as it has entered paralysis. Your head may feel like it was spinning in slow or fast circles, making you dizzy or sick to your stomach. Do your best not to give into these sensations too much.

You may experience jerking sensations that spring you out of this state of being, or hear the sound of a loud electrical pop or snap. Sometimes a bright flash of white light may pierce your vision, accompanying the popping noise. These are some of the things I have recorded personally in my journals.

Womb Meditation

For this practice, you will need plenty of time on your hands and little to no distractions. You may decide to perform this exercise in the dark (recommended) or in very dim candle light.

Your location will be in the bathtub. Do your best to make sure the tub is clean enough for bathing, and fill it up with not too hot of water. If the water is too hot during this meditation, you may burn yourself as you are more likely to fall asleep too. Allow the water level to reach a little less than half way in the tub, as you will end up lying down with your ears submerged under the water. It is okay if you cannot lie completely down with legs stretched forward. Your knees can be bent or legs can be comfortably raised.

Safely place yourself into the tub of water and simply sit down slowly. Move your body to the back of the tub with your legs forward and try to reach your toes. Breathe in before the stretch and exhale during the movement, holding for ten-twenty seconds if possible. Stretch your arms out a bit roll your shoulders and eventually your neck. Gently breathe throughout these movements.

Also, shake and nod your head slowly. By now, you should be used to messaging your body gently and its energetic feel, so do so for this practice. Your body needs to be as loose and relaxed as possible before beginning this advanced exercise.

Now that your body is relaxed, carefully lie down in the tub of water partially submerging your head so that your ears are comfortably beneath the water's surface. Place your palms together in the prayer gesture, relaxing them on your chest. If in the dark, leave your eyes open. If in dim lighting, close your eyes softly. Bring awareness to your breathing and listen to the peculiar sound of slowly inhaling and exhaling under water.

Allow your belly to fill up first, moving the breath upwards. Let it fill your chest area and then release as quietly as possible. Let the rhythm of your breathing relax you even further. Again, once you reach a certain point with your breath work it will seem to get even quieter and your breath will then begin to take care of itself.

As you have probably noticed already, you are able to hear your heart beat. As you listen to your heart beat, focus and feel the sensations practiced in the Heart Beat Transfer Meditation. After some time, the underwater echo of your beating heart should remind you of what you experienced in the womb. As more time goes by, you may experience a tunneling sensation and possible emotional memories from what it was like being in your mother's belly.

Again, do not get lost in the darkness or any

emotional sensations. Simply observe and be vigilant during the experience. Try integrating the Heart Beat Transfer Meditation steps at this point as well. It's likely that you will experience your body subtly pulsing under water, furthering your discipline of awareness.

It's even likely that the sounds of piping, hissing, or humming will return and fade in and out. You may also experience the same imagery and sensation effects from the Dark Waters Meditation.

To pull yourself back to the surface, so to speak, return to the pulsing of your heart in your body, back to the rhythmic breathing, and, if in the candle light, slowly open your eyes. It's very important that you do not jolt yourself out of this meditation because that can result in a short-lived headache, dizziness, and queasy sensation. If in the dark, close your eyes and begin to buzz like a bee or hum yourself to wakefulness.

After this experience, your body can feel very heavy, and deeply relaxed. So, with wakefulness, slowly roll on to your side, and raise yourself up sideways. This is easier on your back.

Lastly, drain the water from the bath tub safely stand up and finish with a quick shower. Be sure to give yourself more lighting and stay safe during the closing part of this practice.

Perform this exercise periodically and remember to record what you have experienced in your journal.

Experience Life More Profoundly

Have confidence, a new you will start to emerge.

Reaching the advanced ability to identify with and understand your feelings is critical in the use of empathy toward others. Empathy with our immediate and non-local environment, people, and all things leads to the greater part of you. Everything has its share of intelligence and awareness. Understanding the mediums within your control via thought, word, and action allows you to experience life more profoundly.

Your awareness and its presence evolve from a potential to an actual cause. This force within you and all around you is limitless. It has no boundaries. The vibration from your awareness moves from the potential, granting momentum then rhythm into all things tangible and intangible; the seen and the unseen. Your boundless principle is without a doubt ready to be directed, but only based upon the quality of your very being.

Making connections and communication is the artful way of the universal principle. Identifying and sharing feelings with others is an important part of building relationships. Feelings are transferred into thoughts, words, and actions. Emotions are the energy behind the feelings and advancing at this stage begins to match up with the golden rule:

"So in everything, do to others what you would have them do to you…"

The idea behind this is that we as humans are born with a will to receive. People universally demand respect, love, and appreciation, whether it is deserved or not. Understanding this desire, Christ promoted the positive command in how to bestow love proactively. You see this idea noted throughout scripture many times and here are just a few more examples:

"Watch ye, stand fast in the faith, quit ye like men, be strong. Let *all* that you do be done with love."

-1 Corinthians 16:13-14

"...the fruit of the Spirit is love, joy, peace, patience, kindness, generosity, faithfulness, gentleness, and self-control. There is no law against such things."

-Galatians 5:22-24

Watch ye tells us to be vigilant during our transformation. *Stand fast in the faith* is a reminder for us to move in faith toward all directions in life. *Quit ye like men, be strong* means to be courageous and strong on our spiritual journeys. Finally, *let all that you do be done with love* teaches us to follow the golden principle in thought, word, and action. If you meditate on and put into practice the things that describe the fruit of the spirit, you shall yield, to the best of your ability, the fruit.

Your supreme struggles with the contents of your

intelligence and heart that can or have sabotaged you are beginning to be subdued at this point. Disciplining the watery world of emotions will help you to find a transformative love of an artful type that you have never experienced before. So far, you will have raised your vibrations and now have momentum for what lies ahead.

For the purpose of our emotional understanding, let us look at chapter seventy-eight of the Tao Te Ching; written by Lau Tzu, a Chinese Taoist philosopher.

"Nothing in this world is softer and more yielding than water. Yet it wears down the hard and strong, and none can overcome it. Though anyone can conquer it; that which is yielding conquers the strong, and soft overcomes that which is hard."

-Lau Tzu

If you observe nature and how it imitates life, you may become aware of emotions and how they imitate water. How is this so? Let us interpret what has been written. *Nothing in this world is softer and more yielding than water.* For the sake of our discussion, we will imply that water represents emotions. Their *softness* constitutes subtlety, delicateness, and fragility. As water yields, emotions also easily give way to other emotions, thereby increasing their density and transmuting into feelings.

Yet it wears down the strong... What and who are the strong? Rocks and mountains are strong, but so are you and I. The human body can be made strong and capable of seemingly impossible things; however, it appears that emotions are capable of also wearing us down. Isn't it interesting that something innately subtle can sabotage our well-being?

Next Lao Tzu says that *none can overcome it.* It is true that we cannot defeat emotion or prove too superior to it, but we are also not inferior to emotions either. Why is that? Well, because emotions are an extension of who we are which also means it is an illusion to see our emotions as separate entities.

However, *anyone can conquer it...* This is true! We can conquer our emotions, but not overcome them. So, is there a paradox? Not necessarily, because although the words are synonymous there is a different meaning implied here. Conquering our emotions and putting them into practice means mastering directional and emotional control.

That which is yielding conquers the strong, and soft overcomes that which is hard. The last part of the verse is a representation of putting to practice the philosophy behind Lao Tzu's words and mastering it. In life, it has been obvious that we face levels of difficulty. Rising to emotional control is part of The Way, allowing us to yield our emotions to conquer life's emotional roller-coaster. If you are able, observe how water flows in a river. The flow comes up against rocks, leaves and sometimes whole trees. Witness how the river yields and moves around the objects, effortlessly.

Now let's deviate from Lao Tzu and refer to an interesting quote from Bruce Lee for enhanced clarification.

"Empty your mind. Be formless; shapeless, like *water*. Now, you put *water* into a cup, it becomes the cup. You put *water* into a bottle, it becomes the bottle...you put *water* into a tea pot, it becomes the tea pot. Now, *water* can flow, or it can crash. Be *water* my friend...Now, you see the idea is running water never grows stale. So, you got to keep on flowing."

- Bruce Lee

Based off our interpretation on Lao Tzu's words, we can again see the astonishing relevance in Bruce Lee's philosophy as well. It is undeniable that water can symbolize emotions, and these are respected forces in nature and life.

Lastly, let's go back to the practice in the chapter on disciplined relaxation and add more practice. If you have cultivated the *water wheel effect,* then by now you should be use to an unblockage of energy throughout your body.

Emotional Flow Meditation

Place yourself somewhere standing outside in nature and on comfortable ground. For instance, choose a nice patch of soft grass or smooth surface to stand on.

With your bare feet, connect with the surface below you. First take the word "fear" and any feeling behind it.

Starting from your heels, begin to embrace the feeling of fear; which is energy. Inhale this energy slowly up through the front of your body and then exhale this energy slowly back down through your spine and to your heels and into the earth. Try not to worry about "Mother Nature", *She* knows what is best for that kind of energy and recycles it well.

Consciously accepting fear into your body and filtering it throughout is a critical step in filtering energy. After cleansing fear from your emotional body, introduce the words *courage* and *strength*. Starting at the heels again, embrace that energy. Again, inhale the courage and strength slowly up the front of your body and then exhale this energy back down through your spine and to your heels and into the earth.

Continue to do this practice with the prominent "negative" emotions in your life, remembering to filter the "positive" emotions as well. If you have not already, try adding certain types of music to your practice. This can influence your atmosphere and make things more interesting.

Try to perform this practice daily for at least 15-30 minutes. Experiment with the differences you experience when practicing this meditation in the morning, day, and night. You will notice a significant change in your connection to nature. Write down your experience and see how else you can form a relationship with the outside world.

Keep most of what you learn practical *otherwise* your spiritual transformation will only remain theoretical.

These practices should reveal more and more bodily/ emotional truth day after day. Remain sincere on your journey and not too serious. This is all supposed to be enlightening and creative.

"If your emotional abilities aren't in hand, if you don't have self-awareness, if you are not able to manage your distressing emotions, if you can't have empathy and have effective relationships, then no matter how smart you are, you are not going to get very far."

- Daniel Goleman

TO INTERNALIZE

Right thought is mastery and it is the airy expression that removes the obscurity concealing clarity. Disciplined thoughts are essential for you to become a person of vision and masterful imagination. The potentially gentle, forceful *wind* directs understanding of who you are as an individual and your place in the world. Improving your clarity means cooperation with all elemental expressions, allowing your body and mind to interact with the alchemical quintessence with increased virtue.

Becoming a technician of the mind promotes greater influence of energy transfer towards wholeness. Having become adept at this stage, you as the fortunate one will communicate skillfully, observe life clearly, and uphold a tangible realization for it.

The operation we are going to work in now is personal separation. This process occurs every time we are faced with important decisions or subjected to situations for the progression of our journey. When we approach this fork in the road, a path is to be chosen.

Sometimes the paths we choose invite failure, but this is only because we struggle to come to terms with the new way of living. Faithfully by now, you should have acquired a certain amount of objectivity and honesty about your strengths and faults. Bringing this kind of justice upon your self will help you to rediscover the essences of who you truly are. You are a gift between heaven and earth.

With your body and emotions, you should be learning to isolate the unnecessary and base elements. Doing this causes you to go beyond certain restraints, and you can begin to break free from outside influences. In your practices, you have been *nursing* your breath deeply and consciously. Breathing this way raises and elevates you toward an enlightened attitude while cultivating spiritual, vital, and energetic awareness. The movements of your hands over your body have become fluid and graceful.

The path ahead of you may not always seem clear, but you must remain empowered by optimistic possibilities, while uplifting virtuous parts of your individuality towards your choice.

So now let us look at an example of the previous *operations*; which also takes us into personal separation: Jonah and the whale.

The story behind Jonah is one of retribution and transformation. Known as one of the oldest accounts in the Bible, the story of Jonah begins with God speaking to Jonah and commanding him to preach repentance to the city of Nineveh.

Let's say that in this story, God represents the individual truth in our lives and Jonah represents you and me. There is always a constant *voice* within us that tries to communicate what course of action would be the best for us to take. However, by our own choice we can either deny this truth or accept it. After being given God's task, Jonah immediately finds this order unbearable. He knows that the city of Nineveh is immoral and corrupt, but it is also a fierce enemy of Israel. Being faced with this fork-in-the-road, Jonah hesitates with his body in going the right way and becomes emotionally stubborn. Can you relate to this?

When faced with our road of trials, like the most of us, Jonah denies the truth of his body and gives into emotional turbulence. Instead of listening to God, Jonah ignores Him and does the opposite. Fleeing from truth, Jonah does his best to attempt to escape his purpose.

I remember times when I decided to escape the tests of life, but you and I know that way never turns out in our favor. There is evidence that our failure to respond accordingly seems to catch up with us. In response to Jonah's flight, God sent a turbulent storm which threatened to ship wreck Jonah's vessel of escape. The terrified crew aboard the boat determined that Jonah was responsible for the calamity.

If we continue to go down the wrong path, we will experience one emotional hardship after another like the storm God sent chasing after Jonah. It is obvious that we use our own bodies as the vessels for escape, involving them in meaningless activities. The crew of the boat can be regarded as the terrifying feelings we undergo. These feelings reprimand us for the lack of responsibility. We always try to do our best to *survive* the unhelpful choices we make by trying to justify our actions. Does it ever work or do we continue to fabricate more falsehoods? Fortunately, for our own good truth does catch up and the universe unfolds as it should.

In Jonah's case, he knew what the crew had to do in order to stop the storm, but they continued trying to *row* to shore. This did not work and the storm grew more violent. The crew was convinced of God's indignation and decided to toss Jonah into the sea to calm the storm. This constitutes Jonah being dissolved within serenity, but still he has not escaped his *Godly* duties.

Instead of drowning, Jonah remains afloat on the ocean and God sends a whale to swallow him up. In alchemy this signifies our point of separation. By *turning away* from his previous decision, Jonah cries out for mercy. He presents with his awareness the need for change and salvation.

Relating to Jonah, instead of drowning in our

emotions we can rush to the surface of being and accept the change that needs to occur. The belly of the whale represents a vessel of operational separation, the universal womb, and the alchemist's platform for metamorphosis. Within our *retort,* we can rediscover our true self and isolate the feelings of reluctance of change.

Jonah remained within the whale for three days and three nights. This shows that time is utilized and patience is practiced thoroughly for transformation. Also consider this, was it not Christ who also spent the same amount of time in His tomb as Jonah did in the whale's belly? What do you think is the correlation?

Released from his struggle, Jonah is *spewed* out from the whale's belly onto dry land. He complied with the command of God by traveling to Nineveh to proclaim the destruction of the city in forty days. Convinced of God's wrath, the people of Nineveh repent from wrongdoing and are spared.

Jonah was angered by God's compassion and left the city to rest. The weather was hot and God provided Jonah with shade, but the next day Jonah became angered again because the shade was ruined. Jonah was scolded for being upset with having the sun beating down upon him instead of rejoicing for the salvation of Nineveh. Now, here is where we need to be reminded of and to understand something very important. The *universe* vibrates everything in its creation.

Practicing our awareness helps us to see our relationship to those vibrations of everything. We are reminded to respect God's process of change; although, we can plan the course of our lives, we do not have absolute control. The city of Nineveh and its people mirror our false way of living, ignoring the truth within us. Jonah becomes the *voice,* warning us of our own demise for not participating in The Way. The universe is compassionate and always provides a pattern for maturity.

If we behave angrily as Jonah did when he did not celebrate the salvation of Nineveh (which signifies the salvation of ourselves) we will continue to match the universal pattern with resistance.

"Do not *push* the *river,* it *flows* by itself."

- A Chinese Proverb

Color Orb Meditation

Art and visualization are more advanced tools that can be utilized to find and reveal the essences of your true self from within. Tapping into our inner artist grants us the ability to become a technician of the mind, increasing the activity of our brain. The mind and brain are not separate, but the mind is not the brain and vice versa. The mind and brain come together to form our *intelligence.*

Do not worry if you feel as though you have no artistic abilities because what I suggest from you does not demand too much talent. However, you may surprise yourself as I have in the past with many projects. Now before we get objectively artistic we must work on being subjectively artistic. Let's start with a simple visualization practice and advance from there.

Return to a quiet and comfortable setting. With this meditation, you may lie down or sit upright and be relaxed.

Your eyes can remain open or closed, however it is preferable for them to be closed. Still your body as suggested from before, breathing deeply, filling your belly gently, slowly. Focus your breath traveling up your spine, then exhale down the front of your body. Do this about three times.

Now, without associating the colors of the rainbow with anything, imagine a red orb suspended in complete darkness but yielding a gentle red glow. Move this orb slightly up then down. Move it side to side, then diagonally, and finally left and right. Make sure to return the red orb to the center of your vision before each movement.

Envision this red orb entering your body through the bottom of your feet, spreading its glow as is ascends. Move it slowly up your body- through your spine, the back of your neck, the top of your head—and then move it down the front of your body. Make sure to inhale and exhale gently following each movement of the orb.

Lastly, imagine this red ball of light stopping and being placed near and at your perineum. This area is located between the scrotum and the anus in males, and between the posterior vulva junction and the anus in females. Now, slowly dissolve this visualized red orb into the body.

Start the process all over and follow through with these six colored orbs in this order:

An orange orb being placed below the navel, dissolving slightly below the belly button.

A yellow/golden orb being placed slightly above the navel, dissolving into your gut.

A green orb being placed at the center of your chest between the pectoral muscles, dissolving into your heart.

A light blue orb being placed at your throat, dissolving within.

An indigo orb being placed at the center of your forehead slightly above and between your brows, dissolving into your pineal gland

A violet orb being placed at the top of your head and visualizing it precipitating down and through your body.

Below is another simple practice I had learned many years ago at the beginning of sensitizing my visualization skills.

Imagine in either your left or right hand that you are holding seven balloons, floating on strings. Each one is a different color of red, orange, yellow, green, blue, purple, and violet. Starting with red one, take its string in the opposite hand and visualize releasing it. Observe in your mind's eye how it floats on upwards toward the sky, maybe passing a few clouds. Let the balloon reach so high that it disappears from view. Maybe you could relate to something you may have seen as a child, watching that lone balloon flee, being blown to-and-fro by the wind and into the atmosphere. Repeat this process with the orange, yellow, green, blue, purple, and violet balloons, in that order.

Do this exercise once a day for at least a week and let each time take anywhere from 5-10 minutes. Remember to remain calm and to breathe steadily throughout the visualizations. Record any feelings, sensations, or possibly other visuals you may have experienced in your journal.

After your week in training, this discipline may guide you towards enhancing and demonstrating future ideas, imagining your feelings in great detail.

Do you remember when you were a child and you watched the clouds drift silently throughout the sky? They sometimes became specific shapes like bunnies or dragons, or perhaps you even witnessed a thunderstorm very intently and your excitement matched the thunderous lightning strikes? I have found that visualizing a cloud as a platform for inner transformation and imagination is very helpful. This works because it imitates nature and it can be formless, at least until the energies you direct and work with begin to take shape. A cloud is easily recognizable and can be simply associated with concepts such as dreams or imagination.

Speaking of clouds and during a thunderstorm, I was about the age of eight and I can recall a very magical memory. My siblings and I were being raised by our mother in Colorado. One night my brother and I had decided to go outside to watch a distant storm over the Rocky Mountains. Lightning was striking high in the sky but it was very quiet in the clouds. The sun and its setting vanished quickly behind ominous clouds. The sky filled up with darkness and flashed with purple lightning streaks. My brother and I were lying on the hood of my mother's car and were amazed at what we were witnessing. Silent lightning filled the sky in the distance and then suddenly stopped.

Sitting up abruptly, we looked at each other in disappointment. We thought that this storm could not have ended this way because it did not feel right. I wondered to myself, imagining how to get the storm started again. So just playing around, I decided to act like an orchestra conductor for the weather. Gesturing and making sounds of an intense classical piece, lightning came again and flashed with my every poke at the sky. My brother joined in with me, as he and I became more and more convinced that we were orchestrating this storm. I was very excited to witness this playful event happening right before our very eyes. Thunder crashed behind and over the mountains with every clap of our hands and the lightning strikes pulsated, veining their way through the clouds and sky.

We motioned for clouds to part in certain areas so that more lightning could be seen, and it worked! In my heart, I felt an excitement and a wonderful relationship being manifested and given awareness to. My brother and I participated in this spectacle for about fifteen minutes or so, and once we stopped the storm dissipated gently.

The passing moments of such an intense experience were yet another influence that furthered my desire to know and understand the magic of the universe. You may discover some interesting, actual effects we have on the environment around us.

TO UNDERSTAND AND ADAPT

"Just as treasures are uncovered from the earth, so virtue appears from good deeds, and wisdom appears from a pure and peaceful mind. To walk safely through the maze of human life, one needs the light of wisdom and the guidance of virtue."

- Buddha

The earthly expression known as grounding breaks the struggle to properly place and articulate you within all precious environments. This virtuous influence reveals rhythm and brings a positive reinforcement to life's ups and downs. Proper composure and necessary silence are key ingredients to enhancing the intuitive strength of your awareness. The earthly essential responses to life are the exchange of virtue, a positive sense of humor, and stillness. These are perfect motives for change, opening many avenues and bringing about significant opportunities. The movement behind the earthly expression is wisdom in action, which uncovers and dissipates the shadows of fatigue and anxiety.

Now, you will enter the more advanced stage of energy work and healing. If you have labored well with all the previous exercises, then I commend you for your applications. You are at a very deserving stage of inner and outer transformation, and this is where you combine all your previous works to produce physical results.

The fruits of your labor will be revealed to you if they have not done so already. Are you prepared to access the intelligence of your heart? Do you feel both the inward pull and outward movement of your awareness, the merger between your soul and spirit? If not, here are the practices for you to gain deeper access to your masculine and feminine ways of knowing.

Extending Energy

We will now work on extending the subtle energies beyond our bodies and into the environment. I would like to make sure that without a doubt you're able to feel the forces that surround the surface of your body. I am referring to the sensations of warmth and cold, and static and/or magnetic flux. Below are the meditations that will help you to focus and sense more of the static and magnetic sensations.

Find yourself a comfortable and quiet location and begin a short 10-15 minute meditation session. You may seat yourself comfortably or stand. Adjust your hands together in the prayer gesture, placing most if not all your focus on the center of your touching palms. Breathe as you have been, but close your eyes for this practice. After the 10-15 minutes keeping your eyes shut, slowly move your palms away then towards one another, back and forth at an approximate six-inch distance. Hopefully, after a minute or so you will begin to sense the subtle connection to a magnetic push and pull between your hands. Without a doubt the force is there, but very subtle.

(Note: if you are unable to sense the flux or static, then it's very possible that you have not actively built up the sensitivity in your hands. This is a must if you are to continue any further. If you are unable to sense the energy between your hands go back to the meditation: *Beginning of Energetic Body Scanning.*)

Do not strain with these movements because the more relaxed you are the easier the connection will be. Feeling the sensations, focus primarily on the subtle field of energy between your palms. Another idea that helps is if you *see* the space between your palms as completely empty in your mind's eye. The emptiness will influence a greater receptivity during this meditation.

Practice this type of sensing for 15-30 minutes every day for almost two weeks before going beyond these expectations. Remember to always take the time to massage your body, and especially your palms. Put more and more awareness on this presence. Log your experiences in the journal.

Being patient and doing the exercises effectuates the cause of your increasing awareness. This also means that you will get results, period. Understand that you are adapting to a hidden field of energy that may be used for a lot of applications. Now, the following stages of practice will discipline the quality of your awareness outside of yourself.

Elemental Work

We will now start to build a physical and non-physical relationship with nature and the ambient energies all around us. One way I have discovered to be very efficient is finding creative ways to work with the known major elements through music and dance. Learning to cultivate the qualities of fire, water, air, and earth will bring you closer to understanding and working with the life force everywhere.

Fire has unique motion and is relatively thin. The size of it can vary: it always offers the idea of expansion. The energy of its flame is bright, electric, and energetic. This encourages strength and creativity, and inspires the idea of perception and productivity. Fire has the intelligence of spirit and it moves outward penetrating the darkness in subtle and massive ways.

Water has an interesting motion and it is a thin but also thick substance. The energy of water is magnetic. It is both calm and violent. On the surface water is compassionate, nurturing, and cleansing. The deeper an individual may dive into the essence of water, the darker it seemingly gets. This journey requires devotion to match the emotional depth of the soul. The essence of water represents the heart as inward drawing and receptive force, but requires forgiveness for how volatile it can be.

Air is dynamic and connected to the thinness of thought, the breath, and wind. With normal vision an individual is unable to see it, but can feel the warmth and cold of its touch. The energy of air is connected to balance, clarity, and independence. The presence of its movement is always optimistic. Wind seeks places to fill which directs the knowledge of the self towards ingenuity and proper use of thought.

Earth is connected to the body and moves in a thick and firm way. The energy of it is electromagnetic, polarized, and enduring.

The presence of earth invites the fortitude of mountains and the stillness of wisdom. Earth is dark and rests in union while concentrating on resolution towards the rhythm of life.

Starting with the qualities of fire, find some music on the Internet through your known media sites or by using your personal inventory that would seem to match its attributes. You know there are all sorts of genres out there, so search for the music that resonates with you. Compile a creative and very interesting playlist. Do this for the rest of the elemental qualities too.

Find an open environment for you to move around and about in. Yes, you will be dancing but with no specific style. You mainly want to work up the courage and execute movement with the chosen selection of music. This will be a great chance for you to be creative and interpret what the vibrations and inspiring sounds mean to you.

Dive into the potential of this unique experience and have no fear. When working with Fire, you could possibly imagine the strength, courage, and expansion of whipping about like electricity penetrating invisible barriers that seem to stand in your way. Perhaps you could move like a single whipping flame that is warm, burning from a candle, and animating your spirit out of darkness.

With Water, you could flow about calmly and softly, nurturing the life, and imagining your force gently flooding into the lives of those who thirst for authenticity. With Air, you could liberate your space, acting as free as imagination. Flowing with your body, pretend to be wind with eyes and ears. You could breeze through distant and make believe sceneries, and explore the life upon them.

With Earth, you could creatively incorporate stillness and movement with every step that you take. Better yet dance and feel the foot prints and impressions that the whole world takes on as everyone starts and continues a daring life journey.

With dance interpretation, the possibilities are limitless. Try not to condemn your imagination to mundane movements. Expose yourself outside the comfort zone of being and express your gift with the music.

This kind of training will lead to advanced relations with your environment and the people surrounding your amazing, creative atmosphere. Try to do this fun exercise as much as possible.

You could even invite others to join in on the experience as well. Be boundless. After having cultivated the qualities of the elements for about a week along with your other practices, let's advance towards evolving your creative awareness even further. Record what you may experience in your journal.

If weather permits, go outside in your back yard or to a park and encounter nearby trees, flowers, grass, and bushes. I am not going to ask you to go around hugging trees and what not, but with your heightened level of awareness inconspicuously feel the textures of nature. See if you can sense that very same awareness you feel around and within your body being reciprocated from nature. Remember that all living things have and share a subtle equal amount of intelligence and awareness.

Perform this practice every day if you can for about 15- 30 minutes. With your evolving conscious and sentient awareness, you should be able to penetrate and nurture the subtle sensations, exchanging virtue and starting to articulate life, vitality, and flow. Again, remember to record your experiences the best you can.

Once you have had some time developing a higher level of sensitivity to the natural, you will be able to participate in skillfully directing the energies around you.

Now, I have always been fascinated by Tai Chi and its artful gestures. For a while I wondered what was really experienced during the movements. I believed there was something more and perhaps something felt. One day while I was standing outside during an early fall sunrise, I was inspired with an idea. As the sun was making its way over the nearby mountains, a gentle breeze blew past my body and indirectly commanded a moment of stillness.

Standing in the green grass, my arms at my sides, I decided to slowly and effortlessly raise them. It would have looked like I was flapping my arms in a very meticulous way, and much to my surprise I had discovered something. Holding a soft focus and relaxed stature, I began to sense a fluid like, invisible thickness all around me. To make sure of what I was experiencing, I decided to bounce my arms gently about half-way up, and felt a subtle magnetic sensation. I was astonished but did not want to lose the sensation by getting lost in it. Discovering this presence prompted me to further experiment with different movements.

The more I integrated the Tai Chi like movements, my awareness of the ambient energies within my environments increased. For instance, I would see and feel the atmosphere around me correspond with my soft gestures. Certain times when I had consciously flexed my awareness, so to speak, the wind would pick up around my body gently and flow about through the grass, nearby bushes, and trees. As the wind would tickle and travel about my body first, it seemed as though nature around me would react the same soon after.

With these kinds of experiences, I had learned to respect the natural world around me, always keeping my conscious and sentient awareness tinged with awe. Of course, I wanted to experiment even more with directing the wind to certain locations nearby. Another idea came to me to utilize the force within and around me and form it into a feeling of pure bliss. With this intangible sensation and motioning with my hands, I then directed the energy of awareness out from the area of my heart towards a tree close by. Holding on to the feeling of unseen thickness, my gesture at the tree proved to be beneficial.

I felt a huge connection and the tree in front of me seemed to wave back, the leaves danced in response with no other movement experienced elsewhere. Once I decided to pass the blissful feeling on and from the tree towards a bush further away, the tree stopped swaying and the leaves ceased fluttering. That bush also waved in a kind response. What exactly was I experiencing? I could not get over the fact that this was happening.

I began to believe with certainly that I was building an interesting relationship to the surrounding natural space. There is an extraordinary force that we cannot see with normal vision and its applications are limitless. I have even attempted to send simple happy feelings to seemingly disgruntled strangers in various environments.

Much to my surprise they would smile and sometimes laugh out loud. These individuals would appear to be slightly embarrassed, looking around for where the feelings had been directed from. There were a few times I was caught, but in return those individuals reciprocated a calm nod or a gentle smile.

Palm to the Sun

With regards to the Tai Chi like movements, one thing I have learned was that getting hung up on how the gestures look was not the purpose behind its practice, even though technical movements usher in certain responses. Instead, the cause of the gentle, soft gestures is to bring you and me to the level of subtlety, to where we can experience the invisible thick presence that connects us to every ambiance.

I will now share with you a practice given to me many years ago during the earlier stages of my spiritual development.

I suggest that this exercise be performed outside as the sun is rising and or setting. What you want to accomplish here is energetic expansion, exchange and enhanced awareness. However, do not feel limited to performing this experiment only at the times mentioned above. It's just that the connection is stronger and easily felt during the sunrise and sunset.

Facing the direction of the sun setting or rising, make sure you are standing with your feet about shoulder width apart for balance. Let your arms be very relaxed at your sides, have your chin up, your shoulders slightly back and chest strong with your butt slightly tucked under your spine. This creates a proper posture which ushers a better energetic flow.

Close your eyes and just be present for a moment. Breathe deeply as you have been practicing and slowly roll your shoulders forward and back in a circular motion. Start to roll your neck gently in order to release tension held there, relaxing your body even more. Once you feel at ease, begin to feel with all your senses one by one.

Opening your eyes and keeping your stance, move your right leg backward and adjust your foot at about a 45-degree angle with your left leg and foot facing forward. Allow your knees to be bent slightly and relax let your arms at their sides.

Now, take your right-forearm with palm facing up and raise it to where it forms a 90-degree angle at your side. Relax in this position for a moment. Next, close your eyes and gently and very slowly inhale and push your open palm forward toward the sun as though you were offering it a gift. Allow yourself to become fully aware of the sensation and movement as you flow throughout this gesture.

Once you have fully extended your arm out with palm facing up, exhale gently and fully. After that, rotate your palm so it is facing down and inhale fully and deeply once more. Imagine you are pulling the magnetic energy through you from the earth in this breath.

With the exhale raise and pivot your palm facing forward then inhale. Follow this with another deep exhale, passing the magnetic feel towards the sun and exchanging the sensation for warmth. Hold this position for a few seconds and begin to inhale the warmth of the sun into your palm.

Feel its radiance being transferred there and with an exhale, let this energy sink into your palm while closing it into a soft fist pointing forward. Next, inhale as you take your extended arm with closed fist and pivot them off to your right side. During this range of motion, breathe deeply into your belly, transferring the energy of the sun from your fist into your solar plexus (right above your belly button in the middle of your belly) and recycle it back to your fist with an exhale.

Inhale gently with the returned solar sensation and begin to move your hand up and over to the top of your head and exhale. Taking that deep breath again; and with your hand raised above, open it and lay it on the crown of your head. Then exhale the energy down through your spine, your legs, your heels, and into the earth.

Now, inhale and allow the sensation of your breath back up into your heels, up the legs passing the base of your spine, and fill your solar plexus with the magnetic energy this time. Move your resting hand from the top of your head and place your open palm in the middle of your belly to transfer the energy back into your palm, and exhale deeply.

Finally, inhale and return your palm to its side and gesture forward once again offering the energy at the sun to be shared, and exhale to finish. I would recommend repeating this practice 4-6 more times, and then switch sides.

Perform this exercise for an entire week each day for 15- 30 minutes to start. Record your experiences. After the first week, you may continue this as a daily practice and if the weather permits.

You may have noticed during this exercise an increase in energy, yet feeling very calm at the same time. Your body might have become a lot warmer and you may have experienced that subtle, thick field of electric and magnetic energy during the movements.

Sensing this energy is the key to evolving your awareness because this is the Chi or Qi (life energy) experienced from the practice of Tai Chi or Qi Gong. Remember that overlapping your passages of perception with feeling greatly increases your chances of experiencing your awareness on very deep, open levels. If you can do this, then you will notice your senses becoming more and more enhanced.

The sensations are only the effects of awareness in

action and that you are not separate from the share of all the surrounding intelligence and awareness. By this time, you would have worked through the alchemical operations of fermentation and distillation, which means that you have begun to master the directional use of energy to transmute and become the greatest vision of yourself. Accessing the deeper ways of inner knowing and movement with both the masculine and feminine energies is what is known as the Sacred Marriage.

As you have worked to achieve intense meditation, you may have already felt the strong desire and motive for optimistic change in your life. By now, you should be working to advance your visualization skills, receiving new insights daily, and amplifying the way in which you live.

Feeling and sensing energy will become second nature, but really it is first. You are truly entering self-mastery and healing and it is my strongest desire that with your growth and new state of awareness you continue the legacy and inspire others on their journey as well.

THE QUINTESSENCE

Realized through reverence and protected by sincerity, the quintessence is the final ascension towards the apex of being. It is the self-substance that is artfully worked with to accomplish the miracles of awareness. It is the ultimate expression that merges healing and mastery. An individual shares the energy and directional power with The All (God, consciousness, the collective, etc.).

As the true power is directed with great ingenuity, an individual can conquer life's initiations and challenges. The adept can inspire others on their journey, offering perspective, focused conviction, and blissful intention. The quintessence circles back to true awareness, establishing faith where its unwavering content molds a firm foundation. This is the final process in alchemy known as coagulation, and equals the formation of the famed "Philosopher's Stone"

Pillars of creative attitude, focus, and loving-kindness are built up and emanate from those who have realized the quintessence. An individual will have unlimited access to the intelligence of their heart because they have traversed the darkness and the light of the soul.

They discover the apex of being by stepping through spiritual doors and into true alignment. All fear has been faced with courage coupled with inner strength. Institutionalized guilt is forgiven and surpassed. Shame and loss are shattered by true acceptance as the reality of being becomes clearer than ever. The lies once told to and believed by one's self have been eliminated.

The illusions of any form of separation dissipate just as passing clouds lose their moisture in the sky. Finally, the need for attachment and the things we have come to love are let go of with a poetic demeanor.

The quintessence may seem like a lofty concept, but it is not. Everything we need is within us and the breadth of a thought away. Creating and believing something to be *too far off in the distance* actually (and unnecessarily) increases the virtue needed to stabilize and formulate your hopes, dreams, goals, and desires. This makes life more difficult than it has to be.

With all of what you have learned from this book, listen to the dynamic whispers from your heart and intelligence. Realize the empowerment in the life that you create and enjoy blissful transformations.

www.ingramcontent.com/pod-product-compliance
Lightning Source LLC
Chambersburg PA
CBHW021233090426
42740CB00006B/506